Read and Respond

A Text/Anthology

Fourth Edition

Janet R. Swinton
Spokane Falls Community College

William J. Agopsowicz
San Joaquin Delta College

Roxbury Publishing Company
Los Angeles, California

Library of Congress Cataloging-in-Publication Data

Swinton, Janet R., 1948-
Read and respond: a text/anthology/Janet R. Swinton, William J. Agopsowicz—4th ed.
p. cm.
ISBN 1-891487-82-5
Includes bibliographical references.
1. Reading (Higher Education) 2. College readers I. Agopsowicz, William J., 1943- . II. Title

LB2395.3.S95 2004
428.4'071'1—dc21 2003043195

Publisher: Claude Teweles
Managing Editor: Dawn VanDercreek
Production Editor: Carla Max-Ryan
Typography: SDS Design, info@sds-design.com
Cover Design: Marnie Kenney

Printed on acid-free paper in the United States of America. This book meets the standards for recycling of the Environmental Protection Agency.

ISBN 1-891487-82-5

ROXBURY PUBLISHING COMPANY
P. O. Box 491044
Los Angeles, California 90049-9044
Voice: (310) 473-3312 • Fax: (310) 473-4490
E-mail: roxbury@roxbury.net
Website: www.roxbury.net

From Jan

To my husband, Duane, my children,
Jennifer and Nathan, and my
mother, Myrtle.

From William

To my wife, Anna, the bratface.

Contents

Preface

To the Instructor

In developing each of the four editions of *Read and Respond,* we have been guided by the same principles: To retain the integrity of teaching reading comprehension through summary writing, thereby strengthening the reading-writing connection and eliminating the uncertainty of objective quizzes; to provide step-by-step models and exercises for systematic progression; and to include varied, timely, interesting articles that students will enjoy and learn from. However, we are careful to make half or more of the book new by extensively revising existing chapters and adding new ones. The Fourth Edition is the most extensively revised edition yet, and we have attempted to respond to suggestions from reviewers, whom we graciously thank.

The look and structure of the book are new. At the beginning of Chapters One through Seven we have placed overview maps. These maps serve two purposes: (1) They allow students to see a chapter's main topics at a glance, reinforcing the all-important preview step in reading; (2) They serve as models for the technique of mapping, which is taught in Chapter Six as one way of recording first reactions and extensively in Chapter Seven as a way to study textbooks. We have also included self-check reviews at the ends of chapters. These function as chapter summaries in the form of quizzes. In these reviews, students will be able to display comprehension of the main points of a chapter and also reflect on the importance and use of chapter contents in their personal and academic lives.

Whereas the third edition had six chapters of instruction plus an anthology, the fourth edition has eight chapters, seven of instruction, models, and activities and one of additional readings. We have also included some group activities along with the individual activities. Working as individuals, both in small groups and in large groups as a class, is a pedagogically sound practice. A special icon () is located next to each group activity to quickly identify it.

Two new chapters open the Fourth Edition of *Read and Respond*. The first contains a general discussion of acquiring language. We have found that many students relate well to it in classroom discussions. This chapter also includes material on distinguishing between narrative and non-narrative writing and reading. The second chapter focuses on vocabulary development. It covers a wide array of vocabulary acquisition, but it concentrates on the importance of learning vocabulary in context.

The separate chapters titled Discovering the Topic and Locating the Main Idea have been combined in the new edition into Chapter Three. This is a logical marriage that is reinforced by our teaching experience.

Chapters Four, Five, and Six improve chapters from previous editions. They systematically teach students to find major details, to write a summary, and to write a response. Each of these chapters includes changes in model essays and clarified instructions.

Chapter Seven, Reading Textbooks, provides new material and improved instruction. An entire chapter from a sociology textbook allows students to practice reading strategies presented in the chapter.

A significant number of the fourteen additional readings for practice in Chapter Eight are new. Furthermore, they come from a variety of disciplines and are primarily representative of college reading assignments. We include both narratives and expository essays for students to experience and summarize. We hope that these essays will help students practice valuable reading and writing skills as well as acquire valuable background information in a variety of content areas.

To the Student

Read and Respond gives you a step-by-step method to improve your skill in reading, summarizing, and responding in writing. The skills you learn and refine in these areas should assist you in school, in the workplace, and in your personal lifelong learning. At the heart of critical thinking, these skills will help prepare you for success in all areas of life.

The opening chapter discusses how you acquired oral and written language skills, and it distinguishes between narrative and non-narrative writing. It lays the foundation for your skill practice in the rest of the book. In each chapter, we provide models for the application of comprehension and summarizing skills. We also include activities, both individual and group, so that you can practice repeatedly. Group activities are marked with a symbol, or icon ( ), and allow you to learn by interaction with classmates.

As with other skills, it takes practice to improve your reading and writing ability. A good tennis player stays in practice by hitting tennis balls on a regular basis; a pianist practices piano at least an hour a day; a dancer rehearses for hours each week.

This book includes a wide variety of selections in each chapter, along with a separate chapter of additional readings. Many of these essays are taken from textbooks such as the ones you will need to study throughout your formal education: sociology, communications, biology, and intercultural studies. Because textbook reading is so important, we also provide a separate chapter on this skill to help you learn and practice strategies for reading textbooks. Chapter Seven contains an actual chapter from a sociology textbook, as well as instruction, models, and activities.

Chapters One through Seven start with overview maps. Use these maps to gain quick insight into the chapter's main points and organization. In Chapters Six and Seven, you will be able to make your own maps either to organize your thoughts or to preview a textbook. At the end of each chapter is a self-check review that allows you to test yourself on the chapter's main points and to reflect on the importance of the information presented.

We hope that your work with *Read and Respond* will prepare you to be more successful in your other classes and in your career. In that way, this book will serve a purpose far beyond the immediate goals presented in its chapters and the goals you and your instructor have for your class. ✦

Acknowledgments

The authors deeply appreciate the encouragement, inspiration, and assistance we have received from colleagues, friends, students, and family. We would like to thank Michelle McGaw for her assistance with the survey maps and many aspects of preparing the manuscript; Karen Benjamin for her generosity regarding the use of articles from Parenting Exchange; and Sarah Powell and Nathan Swinton for allowing us to use their study charts as models. In addition we thank the following reviewers for their helpful advice, which guided us as we made revisions for this fourth edition of *Read and Respond*. Thomas Butler (Paradise Valley Community College); JoAnn Carter-Wells (Cal State, Fullerton); Gretchen M. Cupp (Yuba College); Venita Faler (South Puget Sound Community College); Barbara Fowler (Metropolitan Community College); Jacqueline Simon (Rider University); Billie J. Slocum (Arizona Western College); Priscilla Underwood (Quinsigamond Community College); and Maggie Hahn Wade (Triton College).

Finally, we would like to thank our publisher and project manager from Roxbury, Claude Teweles and Carla Max-Ryan, and copy editor, Ann West, for their help and patience. ✦

Chapter One

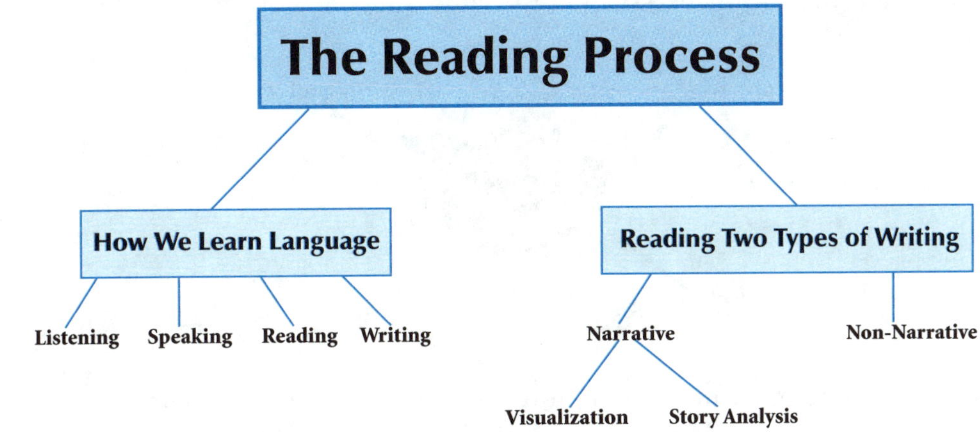

The way we learn has a great deal to do with the reading process. We need to know some language before we can read, but we also learn language by reading. The information in this chapter will help you

- Understand the process of learning language.
- Understand the important role of reading in that process.
- Understand benefits of identifying the type of reading before you read.

How We Learn Language

Most people learn language in the following order: (1) listening, (2) speaking, (3) reading, and (4) writing. In other words, a newborn baby first hears language, then tries to imitate it by speaking. This is accomplished quite easily and naturally for most people, and youngsters talk and understand their native language fairly well at only 2 to 4 years of age. Think about it: children who have never been to school, never completed a homework assignment, have language skills.

A few important lessons are here for us: first, listening must precede speaking. We cannot imitate sounds we have not heard. This means that we cannot usually speak better than we can listen. Second, oral language is based on sounds. Someone speaks sounds, and someone else hears them and understands them. Listening and speaking are, then, really two sides of the same coin, the oral language coin.

Let's look at an example. A child repeatedly hears the word *door.* "Open the door." "Don't slam the door." "Please lock the door." A child understands what a door is (in whatever language is spoken). Soon the child can then say the word *door* and know what it means. Conversation about doors is now possible.

When we turn to written language, the analogy can be made that reading and writing are two sides of the same written language coin.

When something is written, it is put down in code (written symbols that we call letters). A reader then decodes, or reads, them. Again, some important lessons are learned here: just as in the analogy about listening and speaking, we cannot usually write better than we can read. When we read, we see the letters that represent the sounds of the language and connect the sounds and symbols. When writing, we *make* the symbols that represent sounds. In the example used above, a reader must connect the sound of *door* to the four letters that represent this sound in English. We also must realize that reading and writing are more difficult for most people than listening and speaking. Writing is probably the most difficult thing we can do with a language.

Also, the all-important step between oral language and written language must be bridged because we cannot usually read at a level above our oral language skill. Let's go back to the example about the door. Because a child knows the sound of the word *door* and understands what it refers to, he or she can use the word. However, the child still needs to connect that sound to the letters *door* in order to read it. Finally, the child must write the four letters in *door* so that someone else can read it.

The process for learning language can be diagramed this way:

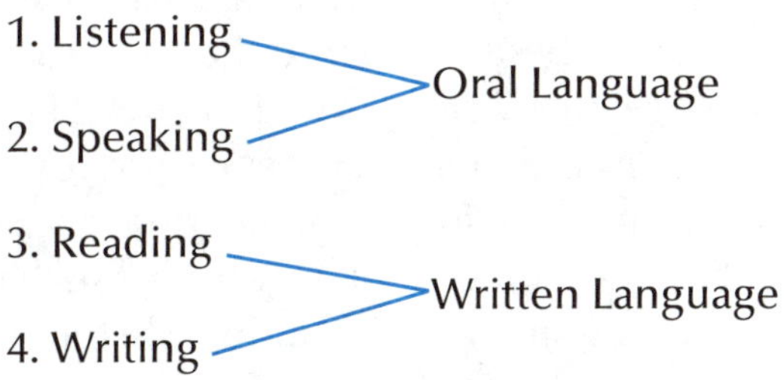

This information may sound very technical, but it is helpful to understand the demands placed upon you to read and write. Congratulate yourself for the ability you have in this area now because reading and writing are the most difficult processes to perform in language. Then realize that you can become a better reader (and writer) by reading. Reading is a free lesson in writing as well as in reading. When you read, you might think you are merely gaining information or enjoying a story, but you are also practicing reading, learning vocabulary, and seeing the written symbols that represent the sounds you know. You are seeing the language spelled, punctuated, and correctly divided into paragraphs. On the written language coin, reading is comparable to listening: it is the basis of writing just as listening is the basis of speaking. Treat reading as a natural, easy way to improve both reading and writing. Enjoy stories and informational articles. You will gain knowledge, become a more fluent reader, learn more about writing, and build vocabulary.

In *Read and Respond,* we offer structured techniques to improve reading and writing skills. However, the number one piece of advice we have is to find a topic you enjoy and read about it. Take advantage of the skill you have and start practicing it by reading whatever interests you.

Reading Two Types of Writing

Authors write for four main purposes: (1) to tell a story, (2) to describe, (3) to explain, and (4) to argue or persuade. Often these purposes are combined: stories contain description, for example, and articles that explain a position (exposition) often contain persuasive techniques. Although it might be useful to differentiate all types at times, such as in a debate class, it is probably helpful to most readers and writers to focus on just two writing types: narrative and non-narrative. This is true because narrative, even if it contains description, is a story or account organized in time (chronology). Non-narrative text is organized logically with main ideas and major details and uses a variety of organizational patterns. If you begin a reading assignment by first determining whether it is narrative or non-narrative, you will have a better idea of the best way to read the assignment.

Looking to see whether writing is narrative or non-narrative is the first step in previewing. Previewing is an important step to improve your reading. This strategy involves looking for meaningful comprehension clues before you read a passage. You will learn different methods of previewing in the chapters of *Read and Respond,* but you can start off by simply determining whether you have narrative or non-narrative material to read.

Narrative Writing

We recognize narrative writing mainly by time markers, words or phrases that indicate time and time shifts. The classic start of a fairy tale is "Once upon a time . . ." Here are other examples of common time markers:

At 10:30 a.m. . . .
Later that day . . .
Ten minutes later . . .

In the morning . . .
After dinner . . .
Before he left the house . . .

EXAMPLE 1.1

Notice the time markers that are in boldface type in the following paragraph:

When I was sixteen years old Patrick Olson asked me out on a date. It was to be my first real date. We decided to go ice skating and then to a late movie. **All day**

long my mom helped me get ready for the big date. However, when Patrick arrived **at six o'clock sharp,** my dad was not there to ask him questions about where we were going and what time he would have me home. It's not that Dad did not want to be there; he just lived too far away.

COMMENT: The references to time as well as the information given make it clear that this is a narrative paragraph.

Sometimes what appears to be a narrative in your initial preview is just a narrative lead-in to a non-narrative essay. For example, read the following textbook selection and notice that it begins with a narrative. However, in the last paragraph, there is a shift to a non-narrative essay. The three-paragraph narrative is a lead-in that provides an example of the point the author is making in the rest of the essay.

EXAMPLE 1.2

David Hoffman and Kathleen McKinney met in the first grade in 1930 in Detroit, Michigan. David's family was one of the few Jewish families in Detroit; Kathleen came from a large Irish Catholic community. David's parents, Joseph and Ida, emigrated from Germany in 1928 and joined a small community of immigrant Jews who were active in the Beth Israel congregation. Joseph financially provided for the family, and Ida took care of the home.

Kathleen's family was active in St. Mary's Catholic church, but she attended Jefferson Memorial Elementary School, the same school David Hoffman attended. . . .

During high school, Kathleen and David started dating. They did not tell their siblings, families, or friends, but they saw each other at school whenever they could. As their relationship became more serious, they anticipated their families would be against their union. Nevertheless, they felt very strongly about staying together, and just before David was to leave for college, they eloped.

Religion is a powerful and pervasive force in shaping families. The 1997 World Values Survey indicates that Americans are among the most religious in the world (*Americans Are Churchgoers* 1998); over 90 percent of Americans indicate some religious identification (Gallup and Castelli 1989). In addition, over 44 percent of Americans, compared [with] about one quarter of British and French, attend church regularly (*Americans Are Churchgoers* 1998). . . .

COMMENT: This textbook selection continues discussing the role of religion in relationships. The story of David and Kathleen is not mentioned again. Therefore, the reader can see that the narrative was a lead-in to non-narrative writing. If a story does continue, we have a narrative, and in order to understand, remember, and summarize a narrative, we offer two techniques—**visualization** and **story analysis.**

Even though we have different learning styles, most of us are primarily visual learners. We like to see things, such as pictures, graphs, charts, and drawings. When we can visualize something, we usually remember it, and narratives provide us with images or stories that we can picture in our heads.

Visualization

One way to remember details of a story is to visualize scenes or "play a movie" in your mind. Try to picture the characters, actions, and scenes. The author often gives visual clues (height, weight, hair color, etc.) that you can put all together in an image you will remember. Also picture the characters doing something—running, working, driving a car, speaking—whatever the author says they are doing at the time.

In the paragraph in Example 1.1 about the 16-year-old, for example, we can tell that the woman is still young enough to be at home and to be assisted by her mother in preparation for a date with Patrick. Few descriptive details are given, but we can fill in the details. Perhaps you picture a 16-year-old girl, with long dark hair, and when Patrick arrives you picture him as very tall and athletic looking, with red hair and light skin, dressed in a suit that is too small for him. It does not matter in this case what the details are, but it is still helpful to fill them in. In a different paragraph, these details might be important. If the paragraph dealt with the girl's concern about how Patrick was dressed, for example, then your images would be crucial.

What is important to visualize in this instance is the mood of the narrator. She calls it a "big date," indicating that she is excited about the evening, and she seems to enjoy the support of her mother. It is good to visualize that, and then to picture her disappointment because her father is not there, apparently because he no longer lives with her mother. It also appears that the girl has a good relationship with her father; she does not fault him for ignoring her, but the circumstances make her sad.

Story Analysis

Stories (narratives) have structural parts that can be analyzed. Thinking about the following parts will help you understand and remember the story:

Setting. When and where does the story take place? Can you tell if it is modern times or the nineteenth century? Does the story take place in a large city or a small town, on a farm, or perhaps in and around a castle?

Characters. Identify the main character(s). Besides knowing who the characters are, it can be helpful to know their relationship (boss/worker, husband/wife, friends, etc.).

Beginning Event (or Problem). Usually a story contains an event or problem that gets the action started.

Plot (or Action). What action takes place? What does the main character do to solve the problem? These are often the major details of a narrative, divided by time markers.

Outcome. Is the main character successful in overcoming the problem? Does the character learn anything from the events in the story? How do you know?

Personal Thoughts. What did you learn from this story? How might you have acted differently than the protagonist? Are there any possibilities for a different ending to the story? (This part is individual and personal, and it is like the response to an article as described in Chapter Six. There are no right or wrong answers to these questions.)

MODEL 1.1: The Parts of a Narrative

Read the following short story. It is an adaptation of a fable attributed to Aesop, a Greek who lived in the fifth century B.C. Then read the comment on how this story might be analyzed.

Double Trouble

In his downtown office, Harry Gordon finished his work for the morning and decided to take an early lunch. He took the elevator down to the parking garage and got into his new, shiny Corvette. He seemed a happy man when he arrived at his favorite restaurant.

Meanwhile, things were not going so well at home, for Harry had two wives. It was legal to have two wives in Harry's time and place, and his wives got along well. However, there was one problem. One wife was older than Harry was, and one was quite a bit younger. This young wife, Diana, wanted Harry to look young and handsome, but Gloria desired her husband to look dignified and mature, a perfect match for the woman she thought she was.

It was hard to tell Harry's age. He had a full head of hair and kept fit by exercising at a fitness club. However, gray hairs were creeping into his otherwise dark brown hairdo. Gloria thought to herself, "Maybe I can streak some silver into his hair when he is asleep, or maybe even pull out some dark ones without him knowing it. He's a sound sleeper, and I'll pull just a little at a time." Diana had secret thoughts, too, but quite different ones. "Maybe I can pull out all the gray hairs while he naps on Saturday or Sunday in front of the TV," she thought.

Each wife put her plan into effect whenever she had a chance. As the months passed, it became evident that each was succeeding. The success was soon thought of as a failure, however, because poor Harry woke up one morning to feel a cold draft on the top of his head. His foolish wives had pulled every hair out of his head, and now neither of them found him attractive. Harry was obviously not pleased with either of his wives.

Setting: It is clearly modern times because of the TV, elevator, Corvette, office building, fitness club, and so on. Often the approximate time is clear; in other stories it is not given, and you can just say "sometime in the past." The place seems to be in a city (or at least a town), for we wouldn't usually find office buildings and parking garages in a rural setting.

Characters: There are only three in this short story: Harry, Gloria, and Diana. In a longer story it is not usually necessary to list all of the characters, but it is important to mention the main ones. In this story, all three obviously need mentioning.

Problem: The problem or beginning event is the wives' unhappiness with Harry's appearance. This sets the story in motion.

Plot: The plot, or sequence of events, is simple in this narrative. Diana begins pulling out Harry's gray hairs, and Gloria begins pulling out his dark ones. Soon Harry is bald.

Outcome: The outcome can be considered a success in one way: each wife accomplished her immediate goal; however, the overall outcome is not good. All characters are unhappy with the ultimate results.

Personal Thoughts: This story, originally a fable, has an obvious moral about being happy with what one has. However, most stories will get you to think more about the characters and events and will allow you to write a short or long response to the story. You often put yourself in the place of one of the characters. This way, you can decide how you would have acted in the circumstances presented in the story. Sometimes you can draw on personal experiences that seem similar to those in the story. You may even want to try your own hand at writing a narrative, true or fictional.

To sum up, try to determine if you are reading a narrative. If you are, use one or more of the methods described above to better understand and remember what you've read.

Non-Narrative Writing

Non-narrative writing is very common. In fact, "once students leave high school, ninety percent of their reading is informational reading. Only ten percent of their reading will be for pleasure" (Williard Daggett, 1990, seminar: Quality in Education: A New Collaborative Initiative and Process for Change, Linden, MI). You typically encounter non-narrative writing in textbooks and essays, and because these two sources are so important to college work, the focus in *Read and Respond* is on non-narrative writing. Most of the models, exercises, and readings in this book are non-narrative because most textbooks and college writing in fields other than literature are non-narrative.

Unlike narrative writing, non-narratives are usually difficult to visualize or analyze using the techniques discussed above. Therefore, charts, graphs, models, and pictures are included in most textbooks and in some magazine essays to help you read and remember non-narrative writing.

ACTIVITY 1.1

Read the following short article. It is an example of non-narrative writing. Ask yourself if you can visualize something you read. How much of the article is information? Work in groups of three or four classmates to discuss ways to remember non-narrative information if you cannot visualize it.

Summer Sun Safety

It's easy to misunderstand the meaning of the SPF labels placed on sunscreen products. SPF stands for sun protection factor and refers to the amount of extended sun protection a product will offer. For instance, an SPF of 15 means that someone who usually burns after a particular duration of sun exposure (e.g., 10 minutes) will burn after 15 times that particular duration while wearing the sunscreen (15 times 10 minutes, or 150 minutes in the above example).

It's important to realize that reapplying sunscreen does not add a prolonged duration of protection. If someone who burns after 10 minutes of sun exposure applies an SPF 15 sunscreen, reapplication of the sunscreen after 150 minutes will not offer additional protection. Parents are sometimes advised not to use sunscreens on infants, but many dermatologists consider this recommendation a little misguided. The truth is that sunscreens have not been tested on small children, so nobody can vouch for their safety and efficacy. Conversely, there is little to suggest the actual application of sunscreen is unsafe for infants. The trouble starts when parents apply sunscreens believing their infants are fully protected from the sun.

Parents should use protective clothing as the main safeguard against sunburn with sunscreen applied to exposed areas. Parents also need to realize that infants can get a sunburn even while in the shade because they are so much more sun-sensitive than older children and adults. The zinc-based sunscreens appear to be well tolerated by most everyone and are thus a good choice for infants and small children. Whether or not sunscreens with a sun protection factor (SPF) greater than 15 offer more protection is controversial, but there is no harm in using a higher SPF.

Reprinted from Karen Benjamin, "Summer Sun Safety." *Parenting Exchange,* May.June 2000, Vol. 3, Number 5, pg. 1. Reprinted by permission.

COMMENT: The article about sunscreen products is an example of non-narrative writing. It is not organized in time, and it is difficult to visualize or analyze. *Read and Respond* offers techniques to understand and remember non-narrative writing. These techniques focus on determining the main idea and the major details of the author and on writing them down so that you don't forget them. In Chapters Three, Four, and Five you will be guided step-by-step in this process. In Chapter Six, you will have a chance to "reply" to the authors, giving your opinion of their ideas. In this way, you can further practice your writing skills as well as your reading skills.

Self-Check Review

1. In what order do people usually learn language?
2. What is the best thing you can do to improve your reading ability?
3. How is narrative writing organized?
4. How is non-narrative writing organized?
5. What are two techniques to understand and remember narrative writing?
6. How can you use the information in this chapter in school, at work, and in your personal life? ✦

Chapter Two

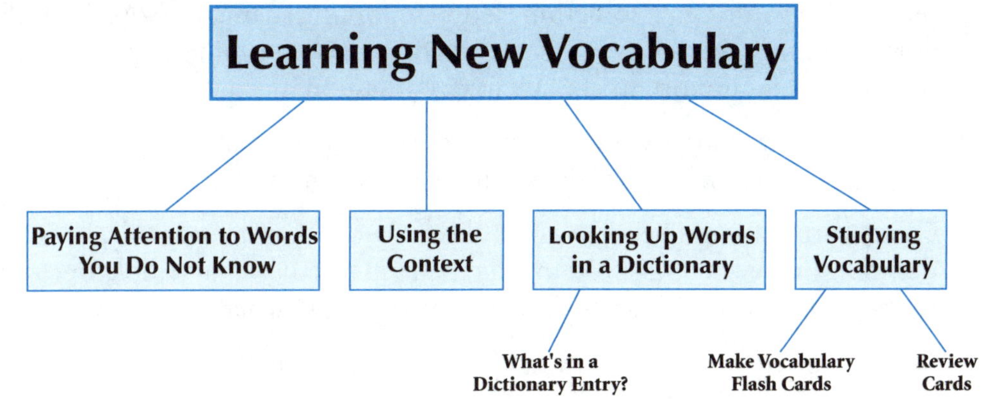

Learning words is essential if we want to be better readers and writers, and we must learn words both by sounds and by symbols. In Chapter One, we discussed oral language and written language, making the point that speaking is usually learned quite easily and quickly. When a child hears words repeated often enough, he or she soon imitates the sounds by speaking them. The models and exercises in this chapter will help you to learn new words by

- Paying attention to words you do not know
- Recognizing context clues
- Using a dictionary to determine the meaning of a word
- Making flashcards

Paying Attention to Words You Do Not Know

A starting point to learning new words is to read, read, read—magazines, newspapers, novels, short stories—anything that interests you. The more you read, the more likely you are to increase your vocabulary. As you read, underline with a pencil all the words that you cannot pronounce AND all the words whose meanings you are not sure of even though you may be able to pronounce them.

Here are a few reasons for underlining new words:

- By underlining a word, you alert your brain that the word is one you need to learn. Although it is too frustrating and time-consuming to stop and look up every word you do not know, it is *not* a good idea to just *skip* the word. Skipping is what we do when something is not important, so unconsciously we tell our brain that a word we skip is not important. Underlining tells our brain that the word is important enough to pay attention to.
- You will find that some words you underline appear in many places, and after a while, you will know what the word is and what it means.
- Other words may not become a part of your vocabulary so naturally, but underlining them will nudge you to look them up in a dictionary, look for clues to their meaning in the context, or ask someone else what they mean.

Using the Context

Context means the words, sentences, and paragraphs surrounding the word that is new to you. Your success at determining the meanings of words from the context depends on the presence of context clues and your ability to recognize those clues. When you speak, you can create a context by pointing, repeating, using facial expressions, and making a change in your voice as well as by the other words you use. In reading, a word may be defined in a sentence by direct definition, pictures, graphs, and the use of synonyms and antonyms. Once you understand how well you are able to learn words by hearing them repeatedly, you will realize how quickly and effortlessly you can learn written words if you read them in several instances. Remember that listening is the key to speaking, and reading is the key to both reading and writing improvement partly because you learn new vocabulary in context as you read.

The following sentences, adapted from *The Essential Sociologist,* by Hess, Stein, and Farrell (Roxbury Publishing) contain different types of context clues.

EXAMPLE 2.1: Definition Clue

> "**Kinship,** or *relationships based on descent and marriage,* was the central organizing principle of most societies before the rise of the nation-state."

COMMENT: Sometimes the context provides you with a definition of the word. For example, the definitions may be highlighted with italics as above or set apart by quotation marks or parentheses.

EXAMPLE 2.2: Definition Clue—Two Terms

> "A third cultural foundation of marriage is based on the principle of **legitimacy,** or **social fatherhood,** whereby one man, the husband, is responsible for his wife's children, whether or not he is their biological father."

COMMENT: Both terms, *legitimacy* and *social fatherhood,* refer to a family situation in which the man is responsible for the children, even if he is not the biological father.

Clues in Examples 2.1 and 2.2 are referred to as **definition clues,** that is, definitions of the word given in the same or nearby sentences. There are a number of ways that authors indicate they are providing a definition. In Example 2.1, the definition of the word *kinship* immediately follows the word and is set off with commas. In Example 2.2, the definitions of both words in bold type follow the terms and are set off by commas. Another common type of context clue is the **contrast clue.**

EXAMPLE 2.3: Contrast Clue

> "By the late 1960s, for many American women, homes in the suburbs seemed as **confining** as they had seemed **liberating** in the late 1940s."

COMMENT: The context of the sentence contains clues that the two terms in bold type (*confining* and *liberating*) are the opposite of each other. If you know the meaning of one of these words, you can make an educated guess about the meaning of the other.

The context may also contain an **inference clue.** Instead of a definition clue or contrast clue, the context may provide a situation or example from which you can logically make an educated guess about the meaning of a word.

EXAMPLE 2.4: Inference Clue

"Women who spent part of their childhood in single-parent homes are more likely than other women to marry early, have a premarital pregnancy, and ultimately to experience divorce themselves. Many of these negative consequences *also characterize children from* ***intact*** *families* where the parents are continually fighting."

COMMENT: The words in italics provide a logical clue that the phrase **intact families** means families that have two parents.

By paying attention to the way a new word is used, you will gain some sense of its meaning. You are likely to start noticing the word in other material you read, and gradually, it will become a part of your own vocabulary.

EXAMPLE 2.5: Context Clue to a Special Meaning of a Common Word

"SIDS: More Research Needed" by Gary D. Compton

Despite some claims, there is no product on the market that can prevent SIDS (Sudden Infant Death Syndrome). However, research has been done that has identified factors associated with the risk of SIDS. One of the most recognized risk factors of SIDS has been brought to the forefront with the Back to Sleep **campaign.** Caregivers are instructed to place a baby on its back to sleep at night and nap time. Since this **campaign,** which started in 1992, the rate of SIDS has dropped 38 percent. Other factors commonly associated with SIDS are soft bedding and second hand smoke. Researchers are also looking into the role that air pollution, coffee, the use of pacifiers, and breast-feeding play in SIDS. Risk factors are not causes of SIDS. However, risk factors may provide researchers with clues to the cause of SIDS and help to identify infants who are most **vulnerable.**

Reprinted from Gary D. Compton, "SIDS: More Research Needed." *Parenting Exchange,* July/August 2001, Vol. 4, Number 6, pp. 4–5. Reprinted by permission.

COMMENT: The two words in boldface type are *campaign* and *vulnerable.* You might be familiar with *campaign* in some sense. Perhaps when you read the word you think of political campaign. The word is also used to describe a series of military actions. In the context of SIDS, the word *campaign* has a related, yet different meaning. It refers to a series of steps taken to combat SIDS; therefore, it is a metaphorical war, but not a literal one. The context tells you that the rate of SIDS has been reduced since this campaign began, and so you can probably determine the meaning of the word in this passage.

With the word *vulnerable,* some context is provided, but not directly. The word is used to describe infants and is in the context of identifying the infants. Clearly the infants need protection; they are capable of being hurt by the disease, and thus they are vulnerable (easily harmed), but you might have had to look up the word to be sure of the meaning. Context clues, therefore, can help you comprehend words that are completely unfamiliar to you or that you recognize only in a different context. Sometimes our worst enemies are words we *think we know, but we really do not because the context is different.* If you learn to use context you will increase your vocabulary and your reading comprehension. However, you must recognize when it is wise to use a dictionary for words that cannot be figured out from the context.

Looking Up Words in a Dictionary

When there are no context clues, you might need to look up new words in a dictionary. Drawbacks to looking up words in a dictionary are that it can be slow, and it often breaks the flow of thought when you are reading. Because of this, we suggest that you mark unknown words as you read, but only stop to look up a word if you need it to figure out the author's meaning. You can go back to your underlined words at a later time to find out exactly what selected words mean and make an effort to add them to your vocabulary.

What's in a Dictionary Entry?

The information about an individual word is listed in each dictionary *entry,* which gives a wealth of information about the word. It is especially important to pay attention to the pronunciation and spelling, the part of speech, and the definition of a word.

1. **Pronunciation.** When you use a dictionary, pay attention to the word's pronunciation. Because English spelling is not always regular, it is important to understand how to use the pronunciation key in your dictionary. Every dictionary uses slightly different symbols, so you need to become familiar with the

key used in the dictionary you are using. A pronunciation key is usually provided at the bottom of every other page or in the front of the dictionary.

2. **Part of speech.** The part of speech usually follows the pronunciation. Frequently, a word can be used as more than one part of speech, so you need to look at the context in which the word appears to choose the correct part of speech and definition. The most common abbreviations you will see for parts of speech are the following:

n.	=	noun
v.	=	verb
vt.	=	transitive verb
vi.	=	intransitive verb
adj.	=	adjective
adv.	=	adverb

3. **Definition.** Most words have several meanings recorded in the dictionary. Therefore, it is important that you check the sentence or paragraph where you found the word in order to select the correct definition. The part of speech can also help you choose the correct definition.

ACTIVITY 2.1

Bring a dictionary to class. Compare your dictionary with those of other students. Choose one word; look at the definition, part of speech, and pronunciation of the word in each of your group's dictionaries. Report on your observations and be prepared to discuss how easy or difficult it was to use each dictionary.

Studying Vocabulary

Sometimes we need to make a special effort to learn certain words. In order to learn these words, it is a good idea to make flash cards. A flash card is prepared from a blank file card. Print the word, its pronunciation, the sentence in which you found the word, and the source on one side of the card. On the other side, write the definition, the part of speech, and your own sentence that uses the word correctly and makes the meaning of the word clear (see Model 2.1).

Making Vocabulary Flash Cards

Flash cards are easy to carry with you, and reviewing them frequently will help you learn the information on them. Look at the front side of the card, say the word, and test yourself by trying to recall the meaning. Then turn the card over to check yourself. Later, do just the reverse; read the definition to see if you can remember the word.

Once you think you know the word, test yourself or have someone else test you on the words by using the flash cards. If you correctly recall the definition, put a check in a corner on the front of the card. Once you have earned two checks, you probably know the word and just need to review it periodically.

MODEL 2.1: Sample Flashcard

Front

kinship

(kin′ ship)

"Kinship was the central organizing principle of most societies before the rise of the nation-state."

The Essential Sociologist, p. 185

Back

Relationships based on descent and marriage

Noun

Own sentence:
Even though there was no kinship, the men considered themselves brothers.

Here are more ideas about learning new vocabulary from actor/comedian Tony Randall in "How to Improve Your Vocabulary."

How to Improve Your Vocabulary

by Tony Randall

Words can make us laugh, cry, go to war, fall in love. Rudyard Kipling called words the most powerful drug of mankind. If they are, I'm a hopeless addict—and I hope to get you hooked, too!

Whether you're still in school or you head up a corporation, the better command you have of words, the better chance you have of saying exactly what you mean, of understanding what others mean—and of getting what you want in the world.

English is the richest language—with the largest vocabulary on earth. Over 1,000,000 words!

You can express shades of meaning that aren't even *possible* in other languages. (For example, you can differentiate between "sky" and "heaven." The French, Italians and Spanish cannot.)

Yet, the average adult has a vocabulary of only 30,000 to 60,000 words. Imagine what we're missing!

Here are five pointers that help me learn—and remember—whole *families* of words at a time.

They may not *look* easy—and won't be at first. But, if you stick with them, you'll find they *work*!

What's the first thing to do when you see a word you don't know?

1. Try to guess the meaning of the word from the way it's used.

You can often get at least *part* of a meaning—just from how it's used in a sentence.

That's why it's so important to read as much as you can—different *kinds* of things, magazines, books, or newspapers you don't normally read. The more you *expose* yourself to new words, the more words you'll pick up *just by seeing how they're used.*

For instance, say you run across the word *manacle: "The manacles had been on John's wrists for 30 years. Only one person had a key—his wife." You have a good idea* of what "manacles" are—just from the context of the sentence.

But let's find out *exactly* what the word means and where it comes from. The only way to do this, and to build an extensive vocabulary *fast,* is to go to the dictionary. (How lucky, you *can*—Shakespeare *couldn't.* There *wasn't* an English dictionary in his day!)

So you go to the dictionary. (NOTE: Don't let dictionary abbreviations put you off. The front tells you what they mean, and even has a guide to pronunciation.)

2. Look it up.

Here's the definition for "manacle" in *The American Heritage Dictionary of the English Language*.

> **man-a-cle** *n.* Usually plural. 1. A device for confining the hands, usually consisting of two metal rings that are fastened about the wrists and joined by a metal chain; a handcuff. 2. Anything that confines or restrains, *-tr.v.* **mana-**

cled, -cling, -cles. 1. To restrain with manacles. 2. To confine or restrain as if with manacles; shackle; fetter. (Middle English *manicle*, from Old French, from Latin *manicula*, little hand, handle, diminutive of *manus*, hand.)

The first definition fits here: a device for confining the hands, usually consisting of two metal rings that are fastened about the wrists and joined by a metal chain; a handcuff.

Well, that's what you *thought* it meant. But what's the idea *behind* the word? What are the roots? To really understand a word, you need to know.

Here's where the detective work—and the *fun*—begins.

3. Dig the meaning out by the roots.

The root is the basic part of the word—its heritage, its origin. (Most of our roots come from Latin and Greek words at least 2,000 years old—which come from even earlier Indo-European tongues!)

Learning the roots (1) helps us *remember* words, (2) gives us a deeper understanding of the words we *already know*, and (3) allows us to pick up whole families of *new* words at a time. That's why learning the root is the *most important part of going to the dictionary.*

Notice the root of **manacle** is *manus* (Latin) meaning "hand."

Well, that makes sense. Now, other words with this root, *man,* start to make sense too.

Take *manual*—something done "by hand" (*man*ual labor) or a "handbook." And *man*age—to "handle" something (as a *man*ager). When you e*man*cipate someone, you're taking him "from the hands of someone else."

When you *man*ufacture something, you "make it by hand" (in its original meaning).

And when you finish your first novel, your publisher will see your—originally "handwritten"—*man*uscript.

Imagine! A whole new world opens up—just from one simple root!

The root gives the *basic* clue to the meaning of a word. But there's another important clue that runs a close second—the *prefix.*

4. Get the powerful prefixes under your belt.

A prefix is the part that's sometimes attached to the front of a word. Like—well, *prefix*! There aren't many—less than 100 major prefixes—and you'll learn them in no time at all—just by becoming more aware of the meanings of words you already know. Here are a few. (Some of the "How-to" vocabulary-building books will give you the others.)

PREFIX		MEANING	EXAMPLES	
(Latin)	(Greek)			(Literal Sense)
com *co, col, cor*	*sym, syn* *syl*	with, very together	conform sympathy	(form with) (feeling with)
in, im *il, ir*	*a, an*	not, without	innocent amorphous	(not wicked) (without form)
contra *counter*	*anti* *ant*	against opposite	contravene antidote	(come against) (give against)

Now, see how the *prefix* (along with the context) helps you get the meaning of the italicized words:

> "If you're going to be my witness, your story must *cor*roborate my story." (The literal meaning of *corroborate is "strength together.")*
>
> "You told me one thing—now you tell me another. Don't *con*tradict yourself." (The literal meaning of *contradict* is "say against.")
>
> "Oh, that snake's not poisonous. It's a completely *in*nocuous little garden snake." (The literal meaning of *innocuous is "not harmful.")*

Now you've got some new words. What are you going to do with them?

5. Put your new words to work at once.

Use them several times the first day you learn them. Say them out loud! Write them in sentences.

Should you "use" them on *friends*? Careful—you don't want them to think you're a stuffed shirt. (It depends on the situation. You *know* when a word sounds natural—and when it sounds stuffy.)

How about your *enemies*? You have my blessing. Ask one of them if he's read that article on pneumonoultramicroscopicsilicovolcanoconiosis. (You really can find it in the dictionary.) Now, you're one up on him.

So what do you do to improve your vocabulary?

Remember: (1) Try to guess the meaning of the word from the way it's used. (2) Look it up. (3) Dig the meaning out by the roots. (4) Get the powerful prefixes under your belt. (5) Put your new words to work at once.

That's all there is to it—you're off on your treasure hunt.

Now, do you see why I love words so much?

Aristophanes said, "By words, the mind is excited and the spirit elated." It's as true today as it was when he said it in Athens—*2,400 years ago*!

I hope you're now like me—hooked on words forever.

ACTIVITY 2.2

Spend twenty minutes reading a magazine or newspaper article. Signal your brain to remember new or unfamiliar words that you come across by underlining those words with a pencil as your read. Remember, you need not take the time to look them up at this point; just underline them.

ACTIVITY 2.3

One by one, look at the context of the words you've underlined (the whole sentence that the word is in and perhaps the next sentence as well). Can you guess the meaning of the word from the way it is used? Are there any context clues? You may want to do this exercise with a study partner so you can talk about the clues you find.

ACTIVITY 2.4

Using the words you underlined in Activity 2.2, decide on five words that you want to know the exact meaning of. Make a flashcard of each of these words. Be sure to write down the part of speech as well as the appropriate definition on the back of each card.

ACTIVITY 2.5

Now, as Tony Randall suggests, use these words several times the first day you learn them. Start by saying them out loud, and then write each one in a sentence (on the back of the corresponding flashcard).

SELF-CHECK REVIEW

1. What are four ways to learn new vocabulary?
2. What are three types of context clues?
3. What are three major parts in a dictionary entry?
4. Describe how to make and use flashcards.
5. How can you use the information in this chapter in school, at work, and in your personal life? ✦

Chapter Three

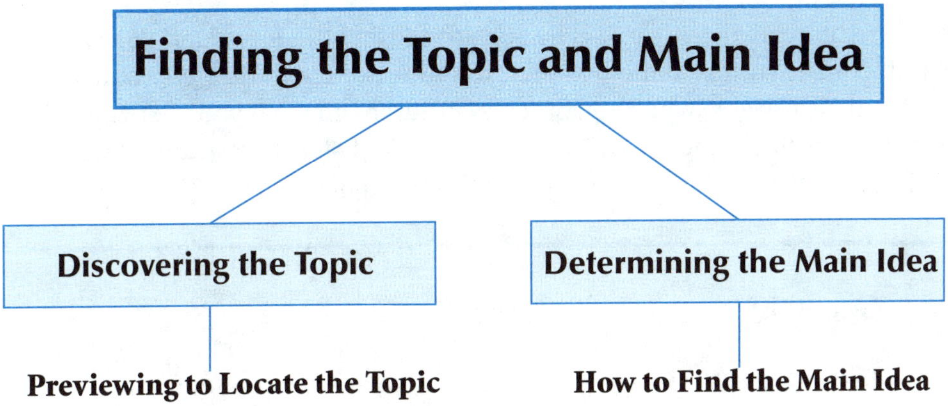

Before you read something, it is a good idea to determine the topic of what you are about to read. **Topic** is another word for subject; it answers the question "What is the article about?" In most cases, you have to know what the topic is before you can determine the author's main point, because a main point expresses an author's opinion about a topic. Once you identify the topic, you can more easily determine the author's main point, usually referred to as the **main idea.** The models and exercises in this chapter will help you to

- Determine the topic and main idea of an article.
- State the topic and main idea of an article in your own words.

Discovering the Topic

A **topic** can be stated in a single word, such as *tests, dating,* or *boating.* These words are very general. The word *tests,* for example, does not reveal whether an article is about taking tests, creating them, or cheating on them. It does not indicate whether the author is concerned with essay tests or multiple-choice tests. *Dating* does not, by itself, reveal if the author will discuss dating practices in different cultures or offer hints on how to find the ideal mate. *Boating* provides no clues to the type of boats being discussed or whether the article is for a skilled sailor or a beginner. There is still much to discover about these topics if you want to know what the article is about.

After you read an article, it is important to state the topic, and you will find it helpful to make your statement as precise and specific as possible. Reading is more useful and pleasurable when you quickly comprehend what you are reading. Identifying the specific topic of your reading is the first step to comprehension.

Compare the general and specific topics listed below:

General	Specific
Tests	Taking essay tests in college
Dating	Dating practices in Mexico
Boating	Boating safety tips for beginners

Adding **specific** information about a topic shows that you understand more about it than is indicated when you state only the **general** topic. To state a topic specifically, try adding information; write a short phrase instead of a single word.

Previewing to Locate the Topic

In Chapter One, we introduced the idea of **previewing** to determine if a selection is narrative or non-narrative. Now you have another reason to preview: previewing will help you discover the topic. Here are specific suggestions for previewing an article.

Begin by asking yourself, "What is the article about?" The answer can often be found in the title, so it is a good idea to look there first. Sometimes the title states the topic specifically: "Steps to Better Listening." If the topic is not specifically stated in the title ("Listening Skills"), you will want more information before reading the entire article. In this case, expand your preview by looking at any pictures, subtitles, and headings and by reading the first and last paragraphs of the article. For more information, read the first sentence of each paragraph. If the article is only one paragraph long, read the first and last sentences. The point is to *quickly* gain as much understanding as possible. When you read with the specific topic in mind, you usually read more quickly and with more comprehension.

MODEL 3.1: Locating the Topic of an Article

Read the following article and look at two possible ways to state the specific topic listed below the article.

Re-Entry Students

Re-entry students have a positive effect on college students, instructors, and the community. They are called "re-entry" students because they have been out of school for a period of time and have come back. Often students take college courses and then leave school for a variety of reasons: jobs, military training, family obligations, indecision about careers. No longer are college classes primarily made up of 18- to 20-year-old recent high school graduates. In many colleges, the average age of all students is approaching 30 years. Occasionally a student graduates from college for the first time at the age of 70 years or older. For younger students, re-entry students are often models of dedication and hard work. Returning men and women help set a mature tone in the classroom, and their life experiences add to the enjoyment of class discussions. Instructors often notice improved student interaction in a class with a wide variety of ages and backgrounds. Students who have had careers in the workplace, the military, or as homemakers add a wealth of information and perspective to a class. Finally, the community benefits from better-educated citizens of all ages. Private businesses and government agencies get workers with better skills and the community gets better-informed citizens and voters. When students re-enter college to improve their lives, they also improve the lives of countless others.

What is the article about? (**Topic**)

The effects of re-entry students

Or you might write,

Re-entry college students' effects on others

COMMENT: There are no pictures or headings, and the title is not specific. However, in the first sentence the words *positive effect* are used. In the last sentence, the verb *improve* is used twice, clearly indicating an effect. Notice that the topic can be stated in more than one way. Reading comprehension is greatly improved when you know the specific topic. From now on, when we use the term topic, we mean the **specific topic.**

ACTIVITY 3.1

Preview the following article and write the topic.

The Key to Good Memory

Good memory depends on interest in the information to be remembered. Most people believe they have a bad memory, but they usually focus only on times when memory fails them, forgetting all the things they regularly remember. For example, youngsters who enjoy baseball often remember batting averages, earned run averages, World Series results, and many other statistics. They clearly have a great capacity for remembering, but they might not remember ages, birthdays, anniversaries, and other numbers important to their parents. People interested in movies remember names and personal information of actors and actresses; those who don't watch many movies probably would not be able to recite this information. In short, interest is the key to good memory.

ACTIVITY 3.2

Preview the following article and write the topic.

Curtis G. Aikens: A Dream on Hold

by Dan Rather
from *The American Dream*

Curtis Aikens, who grew up in rural Conyers, GA, puts a face to one of those literacy statistics we hear, but sometimes cannot believe: he went through high school and five semesters of college without learning how to read. One of the millions who fall through the cracks and keep falling, Aikens believes that he would have disappeared completely if he hadn't, at 26, finally asked for help. Of his literacy tutors, Aikens says, "They didn't change my life. They saved my life."

Aikens put his new skills to good use. A lifelong lover of cooking and food, he started his own produce company in his hometown, became a food columnist and began to focus on his version of the American Dream: "I said to myself, 'I'm going to become a celebrity.'" But it wasn't fame alone he was pursuing, he explains. "It was so, when I talk about the fact that I couldn't read, other non-reading adults will say, 'If he can do it, I can too!'" Today, Aikens has three cookbooks to his name and appears on *Calling All Cooks* on the Food Network. But, he says, he hasn't reached his goal. "I'm still trying to obtain the American Dream, because I want to give everybody the ability to read. I know that sounds hokey, but there it is."

ACTIVITY 3.3

Preview the following article and write the topic.

Do the Facts Ever Lie?

In many controversial articles, there is one set of facts, but two different interpretations. The readers of such articles must question both the facts and the interpretations and make up their own minds. Good readers think and read critically; they do not blindly accept someone else's conclusions.

A study by the National Center for Health Statistics is a good example of why critical thinking is so important. The study concludes that children in nonsmoking households are likely to be healthier than children who live with smokers. The study shows that 4.1 percent of young children in households with smokers were in fair to poor health. Only 2.4 percent of the children never exposed to tobacco smoke were in fair to poor health. However, this conclusion is disputed by the tobacco industry.

The claim by the tobacco industry is that the difference is really one of income levels. In other words, they believe that the study does not take all factors into consideration. It is unfair, they say, to single out smoking as the big cause of the health problems.

The two sides in this dispute are using the same facts, but are interpreting them differently. Therefore, it is up to the readers to question all aspects of the controversy. They need to ask a number of questions: "What is the bias or motive of the tobacco industry in this case?" "Why would a government agency interpret statistics this way?" "How was the study conducted?" "Are there other reasons why these children have poorer health?" These and other questions must be asked in order to make a judgment about such a dispute. Good readers evaluate information; they do not just accept it.

Determining the Main Idea

The **main idea** of an article is the major point the author makes about a topic. In an article, the main idea is often called the **thesis statement.** In a paragraph, the main idea is often called the **topic sentence.**

The difference between the main idea and the topic is that the topic is an incomplete thought that does not show an opinion. The main idea, on the other hand, is a complete sentence that states an opinion. Although the topic may be specific, it does not reveal the author's main point. Notice how much clearer and more complete the main ideas become when information is added.

Topic (subject)	Main Idea (opinion)
The Internet	is a useful research tool.
School uniforms	should be mandatory in K-12 schools.
Professional athletes	should not be paid so highly.
Spanking children	is a form of child abuse.
Anti-cigarette ads	are ineffective.

Note that the word order can often be changed. For example, one might write

A useful research tool	is the Internet.
A form of child abuse	is spanking children.

ACTIVITY 3.4

Extend the following topics into main idea statements by writing complete thoughts that express an opinion about the topic.

The Internet	________________________
School uniforms	________________________
Professional athletes	________________________

The main idea is the author's point about the topic. In examples shown below, the topic is written in italics and the author's opinion is shown in boldface type. Notice that the opinion can be stated before or after the topic.

Knowing how to take essay tests **is a useful skill in college.**

Dating practices in Mexico **are considerably different than those in the U.S.**

Before driving a boat, a person needs to know some basic *boating safety tips.*

How to Determine the Main Idea

To find the main idea, ask, "What is the author's main point about the topic?" To answer this question, begin by looking at the clues that helped you identify the topic (the title, headings, pictures). For further clues, read the first and last paragraphs of the article (or the first and last sentences of a short article), because authors often state the main idea near the beginning or end of an article. If you find a sentence that states the main idea, underline it. Often the main idea is not stated in one sentence. You may have to write it yourself. Even if it is stated, rewrite it *in your own words* to be sure you understand it.

Whether you rewrite a sentence by the author or write your own main idea sentence, you need to read the article to discover if you have correctly identified the

Tips for Writing Main Idea Statements

1. It is important that the sentence you write be a *complete sentence*. A complete sentence contains a subject and a verb, and it expresses a complete thought.

   Complete:
   Knowing how to use the Internet sources can help students succeed in college.

   Not Complete:
   Internet sources and college student success.
   Using Internet sources to succeed in college.
   How using Internet sources can help students succeed in college.

2. State the main idea directly; don't announce the topic.

   Statement of main idea:
   Knowing how to use Internet sources can help students succeed in college.

   Announcement of topic: (not a statement of main idea)
   The main idea of this article is about how Internet sources can help students be successful in college.

main idea. If you are correct, most of the information in the article will in some way describe, explain, or offer examples of the main idea. In this regard, it might help to remember that the main idea is sometimes called the **controlling idea.** This makes sense because the main idea *controls* the details and examples the author selects for the article. If most of the information does not relate to the main idea statement you have written, you should write a **new main idea** sentence based on your careful reading of the article.

MODEL 3.2: Determining the Topic and Main Idea of an Article

Read the following article and look at two possible ways to state the topic and main idea listed below the article.

Taking Tests

What is the first thing you do when you take a test? If you are like most students, you probably start by answering the first question, then proceed through the test, answering the rest of the questions in order. However, there is a better way. *If you follow a few simple steps, you can make test-taking easier and improve your grades.*

The first step is to preview. Spend a few minutes scanning the test to find out how many questions there are and what types of questions are asked (multiple choice, true-false, essay, etc.). Pay attention to all directions. Notice how many points are assigned to different questions or sections. With this information in mind, next make a plan of how much time to spend on each question of the test and of which questions to answer first. Allow more time for sections worth the most points.

The third step is to begin with the section that is easiest for you. This will insure a few quick, easy points for you and will probably give you a positive feeling that will help get you through the test. Confidence is important to good performance on a test, and tackling questions you know the answers to will help your confidence.

Finally, when you come to questions that you cannot answer or are unsure about, skip them for the time being. After you have finished the rest of the test, you can come back to these questions, try to answer them, or guess if there is no penalty for guessing.

What is the article about? (**Topic**)

The value of a test-taking system

Or you might write,

A good procedure for taking tests

What is the author's main point about the topic? (**Main Idea**)

A test-taking system can help you get better grades.

Or you might write,

You can get better grades on tests if you follow four easy steps.

MODEL 3.3: Determining the Topic and Main Idea of an Article

Here is another excerpt from Dan Rather's book, *The American Dream*. Read the article, then study the sample topic and main idea statements that follow the article.

A Troubled Young Man With an Odd Premonition About His Future

by Dan Rather
from *The American Dream*

Wayne Ford was in eighth grade when a teacher asked the class to write their obituaries. How would they like to be remembered? Ford, who lived in a rough area of Washington, DC, came up with a curious response: he said he would make his mark in the Midwest. He would be active in politics and in charge of a community center.

Wayne Ford would go on to get in trouble in high school. "I was doing drugs, robbing, breaking into apartments," he recalls. To get away, he accepted a football scholarship to a small, nearly all-white Minnesota college. Once there, however, racism threatened to throw him off course. Instead, he turned his anger to activism and founded the school's black student union.

"Then," he says, "it all started to come together. The worst things in my life were the things that had the potential to make me great." Ford devoted himself to academics. History especially gave him a new perspective. "When I started reading it," he says, "I thought, 'My God, the world has gone through hell, not just Wayne Ford.'"

After graduation, Ford turned to politics. Today, he's living the dream he had as a boy: he's the only black member of the Iowa State Legislature and the founder and executive director of Urban Dreams, a nonprofit community program for at-risk youth. Last year, he spoke before the Democratic National Convention. It was one of the biggest achievements of his life, but he says, "It wasn't the cherry on the ice cream. The best is yet to come."

What is the article about? (**Topic**)

A troubled boy who had a positive vision about his future

Or you might write,

A boy who used his dreams to turn his anger into activism

What is the author's main point about the topic? (**Main Idea**)

Wayne Ford's vision of himself as a positive contributor to society when he was in junior high helped him overcome his anger and troubles in school.

Or you might write,

Wayne Ford overcame his troubled school years and became an important policy maker by following his dream.

ACTIVITY 3.5

Preview the following article to determine the topic and main idea. After your preview, underline the main idea sentence(s). Then, write the main idea in your own words.

Dyslexia: Recognizing Shapes, Not Sounds

by Sarah Vandershaf

Read these words. You probably can almost hear them as you read. Dyslexics, however, may lack this inner ear for language, making reading more difficult for them than it is for most people.

A preliminary study by psychologist Karen Gross-Glenn and others has shown differences in the patterns of brain activity in dyslexic and nondyslexic readers. The researchers pinpointed 60 structures throughout the brain thought to be involved in aspects of reading—eye movements, language and memory, among others—and measured their activity in six dyslexic and eight nondyslexic readers.

Gross-Glenn and her colleagues found that reading stimulates different regions in dyslexics' brains than it does in the nondyslexics. In both groups, visual regions in the brain were activated. But dyslexics' brains showed less activity than the others' in the posterior peri-insular cortex, a region important for interpreting the sound of words.

The pattern of activity in the dyslexics' brains did resemble that of one group of nondyslexics that the researchers also studied; five people who viewed pictures, but did not read. This leads Gross-Glenn to believe that these dyslexics recognize words by how they look, not by how they sound.

"Many dyslexics read holistically," says Gross-Glenn. "They look at the 'envelope' of the word, the overall configuration." In this way, a dyslexic person could easily confuse a word like "publish" with "polish," since the two are very similar in their outward "shape."

Gross-Glenn also found differences in brain activity among the dyslexics themselves, perhaps reflecting different subgroups of dyslexia. Nonetheless, she is already applying her findings in remedial-reading programs that she hopes will help many types of dyslexics overcome their difficulties with the written word.

Karen Gross-Glenn, Ph.D., is at the University of Miami School of Medicine. She and her colleagues presented this research at a meeting of the Society for Neuroscience.

ACTIVITY 3.6

Preview the following article to determine the topic and main idea. After your preview, underline the main idea sentence(s). Then, write the topic and main idea in your own words.

The Tyranny of the "Shoulds"

by Carol Willmett, L.C.S.W.

We have a lot of "shoulds" that we must meet in order to believe ourselves to be "good." As parents, partners, and friends, we lay pressure on ourselves and others to strive for perfection. Often, the "shoulds" are demands we place on ourselves because of childhood teachings, ideals promoted by our society, and images set forth by the media.

In my work with individuals and families, I have watched with dismay as people flog themselves with their "failures" because they have numerous "shoulds," many of which are not realistic. For example, a woman may feel guilty if she is unable to achieve the perfect body and calls herself "lazy." She may be criticized if her home is not clean. A man may be embarrassed to admit his wife is smarter or makes more money then he does because a man "should" be the primary breadwinner. Others may push themselves to provide their children with opportunities such as dance or gymnastic classes or clothes as expensive as those their peers wear, even if it creates hardship on other family members.

I use a simple technique, which others have found helpful. I do not argue with the Ten Commandments as "shoulds," as many people rely on basic biblical teaching as their moral as well as legal standard of behavior. Indeed, our laws are based on that standard (thou shalt not kill, steal, lie, et al.). Anything else, however, is subject to the challenge of changing the "sh" to a "c."

Shifting from "should" to "could" affects the feelings conveyed from a mandate to a choice. I *could* lose weight, make more money, become more organized, etc., feels much less critical and judgmental than the same expression as *should*. Guilt and resentment are greatly lessened by this simple change.

Just as many of us learned to be self-critical from our parents, we pass those attitudes on to our own children. Telling a child, "You should be more interested in school, should want to share your toys, or should want to play with your brother (even if he is a pain!)" sets up the child whose feelings are not "ok" to feel angry or to feel like a failure.

I encourage you to try this simple exercise. If you are able to become more accepting of yourself, you will also be less critical and demanding of others. Life can become much more enjoyable.

"The Tyranny of the 'Shoulds,'" by Carol Willmett, L.C.S.W. *Parenting Exchange*. July-August 2001, Vol. 4, No. 6, pg. 3. Reprinted by permission.

ACTIVITY 3.7

Preview the following article and write the topic. If you can determine a main idea sentence from the preview, underline it. Then state it in your own words. If you do not find a main idea sentence, read enough of the article to determine the main idea before writing it in your own words.

Test De-Stress

by Keith Blanchard

It's exam period, and you feel as if you're in a movie: The Exams That Ate My Life. *You can't even read the back of a cereal box without highlighting the salient points. Are you going insane? More important, are you going to pass? Here's a handy guide to get through exams with your mind—and GPA—intact.*

Emotions in Motion

While a little anxiety can be good for you (it pumps up your adrenaline and helps focus your attention), when stress starts to interfere with studying or with taking an exam, it's time to take action.

Pre-test Stress

Feeling angry, depressed, restless, or nervous around test time can be a result of negative self-instructions. According to Linda Locher, Ph.D., director of Counseling and Psychological Services for the University of Rochester, "We all have self-image messages we subconsciously play in our head. I call them 'muzak tapes.' At exam time they're usually along the lines of 'I hope I do well.' But for the highly stressed person, the messages become 'I'm stupid,' or 'I'm going to fail.' The key is to recognize these negative messages and replace them with coping ones. Whenever you think, 'This is too hard,' or 'I'll never get through this,' counter these thoughts with, 'This may be hard, but I didn't get here by luck,' or 'I may not be a genius, but I can pass a calculus test.' "

Mid-test Stress

"If you don't manage your stress well *during* an exam, it can build until you really can't perform at all," claims Dr. Locher. And that makes you susceptible to "dumb errors," like leaving out parts of an answer or misreading a question. To combat mid-test stress, stop and close your eyes for a second between questions, blank your mind, and you'll be more receptive to the new question. Try to focus on a pleasant image: You're lying on a beach in Mazatlan with a diploma curled between your toes. "Sometimes it helps just to rephrase the question in your own words," claims Pam Reynolds,* a senior at Spencer-Van Etten High School in New York. "Teachers and professors try to make the questions sound tougher than they are."

Physical Stress Busters

Many students mistakenly view the physical symptoms of stress, which range from sweaty palms to headaches, nausea, and diarrhea, as unrelated to the stress itself. "As if I didn't have enough on my mind with this Pig Latin 201 exam, now I have to get sick, too!" But if exams make you barf, it may be because you're giving your mind a workout but neglecting your body. In other words, you can't just sit in your room with your eyelids stapled up, highlighting textbooks and shoveling pizza into your mouth. Larry Merkel, M.D., staff psychiatrist, Student Health Service at the University of Pennsylvania, offers some tips for keeping your body from falling apart during exams.

Brain Food

Try eating six mini-meals instead of three large ones, since big meals make you sleepy. In terms of *what* to eat, protein (yogurt, peanut butter, cheese) is your best bet because it gives you long term energy. Sugar (Ding Dongs, chocolate bunnies) gives you energy, but the "sugar high" is deceptive because you crash soon afterward. You should also avoid OD-ing on carbohydrates, such as pasta and bread. They bog you down, making sleep more attractive than studying. And speaking of sleep, caffeine does help you stay up late, but unfortunately, large amounts affect your cognitive ability, making it harder to learn new things—so if you absolutely need coffee to stay awake, drink no more than three or four cups in a 24-hour period, and wait an hour or two between "doses."

Mental Floss

There are two types of study breaks—short ones and long ones—and you need both for efficient studying. Short breaks let your mind take a breath and should be taken often. "Find out your study attention span (usually 45-60 minutes)," advises Dr. Merkel, "and take a two- to five-minute break ten or 15 minutes short of that. Waiting until you're exhausted wears down your system and builds up frustration." You should also take slightly longer breaks, say 15 to 20 minutes, every three hours.

Let's Get Physical

Jogging your memory isn't enough. It's also important to get regular exercise during exam time. According to Dr. Merkel, a quick 20-minute workout every day or so will keep your body in tune and keep anxiety tuned out. And it will help you sleep better.

Stay Up or Hit the Sack?

You can't stay up three nights before the exam and expect to do well. "Sleep deprivation really takes its toll," claims Dr. Merkel. "Some sleep is always better than none." There's no minimum requirement of sleep, though you should try to maintain your normal sleeping habits. And if you are forced to pull an all-nighter, don't do it more than one night in a row and try to work in at least a two-hour nap the next day.

Practical Tips for the Practically Ready (and the Hopelessly Unprepared)

Before the Exam

1. *Know your exam schedule.* This will help you spot scheduling problems and give you an idea of when to do your studying. Claims Dr. Merkel, "Some students spend all their energy studying for their first exam and find they're too exhausted afterward to continue at the same pace."
2. *Find out what you can about each exam.* How long is it? Can you bring a calculator? Is it multiple choice, fill in the blanks, or essay? Consult old tests (if available), talk to people who've taken the course, or ask the professor. It will help you organize your studying and make you more confident.
3. *Make up study cards.* Summarize the important points from lectures, readings, and old tests into a few study sheets organized so you can quiz yourself. Just making up the cards lets you run through the stuff once, plus you won't have to lug books around to study.
4. *Choose study partners carefully.* Study groups are helpful if you have a fairly good grasp of the material. They're a waste of time if you haven't even begun to study.
5. *Set your alarm clock.* Every school counselor tells the *hilarious* story about the student who stayed up all week and then slept through the test. Nobody ever laughs.

On Exam Day

1. *Eat light.* The old advice about eating a big breakfast before an exam is wrong, according to experts: It sends blood to your stomach instead of to your head, where you really need it. You should eat a moderate-sized breakfast a few hours before the test, so you can have time to digest your meal.
2. *Relax.* Take a deep breath; let your heart slow down. You have plenty of time. You know this stuff. Look at the doofus over there *still* cramming. Thank heaven you're not him.
3. *Do what you know first.* Get all the guaranteed points you can, then come back to the difficult questions. It builds confidence and opens up the right sections of your mind, which will help you remember things you think you don't know.
4. *If you have a question, ask.* Your professor or teacher might be able to rephrase the question in a way that makes more sense.

Keith Blanchard is a freelance writer/editor living in Summit, NJ.

Note

* Name has been changed.

"Test De-Stress" by Keith Blanchard. From *Young and Modern (YM)*, May 1990. Reprinted by permission.

Self-Check Review

1. What are the steps for locating the topic of an article?
2. What is the difference between a general and a specific topic? Which do you use for the topic of your reading? Why?
3. What are the steps for determining the main idea?
4. How is the main idea different from the topic?
5. How can you use the information in this chapter in school, at work, and in your personal life? ✦

Chapter Four

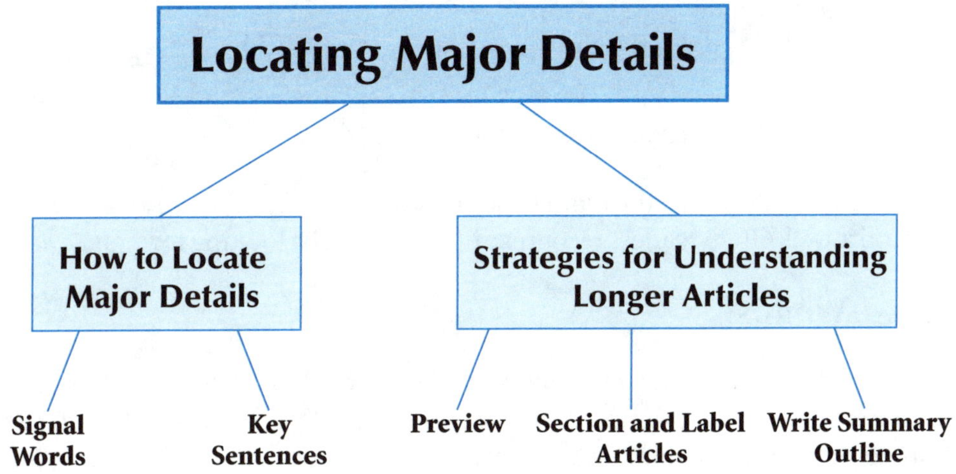

You have a natural curiosity that makes you want to understand both an author's point and the reasoning or support for that point. This sense of curiosity can be developed, and it is essential to critical thinking. Only by examining an author's logic can you intelligently agree or disagree with the main point.

The models and exercises in this chapter will help you to

- Locate the major details of an article.
- Restate the major details of an article in outline form.

How to Locate Major Details

Major details answer the question "How does the author support the main idea?" Authors use facts, examples, explanations, scientific proof, or combinations of these to support and clarify the main idea of an article.

A simplified outline of an article might look something like this:

Topic
Main Idea
- Major Detail
  - Facts, examples, explanation
- Major Detail
  - Facts, examples, explanation
- Major Detail
  - Facts, examples, explanation

If you know the topic, the main idea, and the major details of an article, you understand it well. Often readers recognize major details by looking for signal words.

Signal Words

Major details are often indicated by **signal words and phrases** (sometimes called **transitions**). For example, the word *finally* usually indicates that the author is about to state the final point. In the sentence you just read, the signal phrase *for example* is used to indicate that an example follows.

The following signal words and phrases are grouped according to their function. This list is not a complete one, but looking at these examples will help you learn to identify signal words.

EXAMPLE 4.1: Examples of Signal Words

Words That Signal Time or the Order of Importance

first	finally	before
in the first place	when	after that
second	then	later on

Words That Signal Contrast or an Opposite Point

however	in contrast	despite
but	by contrast	although
on the contrary	in spite of	nevertheless

Words That Signal the Conclusion of an Idea

in conclusion	to sum up	finally
therefore	in short	as a result
consequently	in summary	

Words That Signal the Same or a Similar Idea

and	more than that	likewise
furthermore	also	similarly
moreover	in the same manner	

Words That Signal Causes and Effects

because	due to	consequently
since	therefore	as a result

CAUTION: Read carefully: do not assume that behind every signal word is a major detail. Sometimes an author signals new major details with key sentences or by starting a new paragraph.

ACTIVITY 4.1

Skim (read very quickly) an article from a daily newspaper or news magazine, looking for signal words and phrases. Underline any signal words you find. With two or three classmates, determine if the words or phrases signal major details.

Once you have identified the main idea of an article, you will want to identify the major details. Because signal words often help identify major details, it is a good idea to underline them. In the following model, the sentence that is underlined expresses the main idea, and the signal words or phrases that help identify major details are in bold print.

MODEL 4.1: Locating Major Details With the Help of Signal Words

Read the following article and notice the signal words and phrases that indicate major details.

Improving Your Memory

Paragraph One How is your memory? It is probably only when your memory fails that you think about it. An occasional lapse is normal. *The key to "managing" your memory and improving it is to understand how memory works.*

Paragraph Two **First,** in order to remember something, you need to have sensory input, that is, a sensation needs to be recorded by one of your senses. For example, a plane flies over your house and you hear it, or a cake is burning in the oven and you smell it.

Paragraph Three **However,** sensory input is not enough. Your eyes and ears might be seeing and hearing numerous sights and sounds, but you can only focus on a few at any one time. The ones you focus on are the ones you are most likely to remember.

Paragraph Four **Furthermore,** to improve your memory retention, you must consciously intend to remember certain sights, sounds, smells, or other stimuli and then focus on them. For example, at a party, you might be introduced to several people. If you feel it is important to remember their names, focus on their names and faces and make an effort to remember them. If necessary, use word associations to help you remember. Without the intention to remember, you probably won't retain the name in the first place. Or you may forget it as soon as you hear it because you did not make any special effort to remember.

Paragraph Five **Although** conscious effort is necessary, it is not enough for lasting memory. You will not remember the sensory input for very long if you do not do something to place it in your long-term memory. You also need to review the new information within 24 to 48 hours to remember it over time. Periodic review will ensure that you never forget the information.

Paragraph Six **In conclusion,** improving your memory by using this technique is not difficult. Practice it often to improve your retention skills. Pay attention to the input, your intent to remember, and, of course, review. You have the power to remember anything you want—if you choose to.

COMMENT: The title provides the topic, and the main idea of the entire article is stated in the first paragraph. Paragraphs two, three, and four each contain one major detail. Paragraph five has two signal words, but only one major detail because *although* signals a transition from paragraph four, *also* does not signal a new idea. Paragraph six (the conclusion) restates the main idea and major details.

MODEL 4.2: Locating Major Details With the Help of Signal Words

You read "Taking Tests" in Chapter Three. Read it again here, noticing the signal words in boldface type that indicate major details.

Taking Tests

What is the first thing you do when you take a test? If you are like most students, you probably start by answering the first question, and then proceed through the test, answering the rest of the questions in order. However, there is a better way. If you follow a few simple steps, you can make test-taking easier and improve your grades.

The **first** step is to preview. Spend a few minutes scanning the test to find out how many questions there are and what types of questions are asked (multiple choice, true-false, essay, etc.). Pay attention to all directions. Notice how many points are assigned to different questions or sections. With this information in mind, **next** make a plan of how much time to spend on each question of the test and of which questions to answer first. Allow more time for sections worth the most points.

The **third** step is to begin with the section that is easiest for you. This will insure a few quick, easy points for you and will probably give you a positive feeling that will help get you through the test. Confidence is important to good performance on a test, and tackling questions you know the answers to will help your confidence.

Finally, when you come to questions that you cannot answer or are unsure about, skip them for the time being. After you have finished the rest of the test, you can come back to these questions, try to answer them, or guess if there is no penalty for guessing.

A summary outline of this article would look like this:

Topic: Test-taking made easier

Main Idea: Four easy steps can help you earn better test scores.

Major Detail: Preview before answering

Major Detail: Plan how to use your test time

Major Detail: Begin with easiest section of the test

Major Detail: Temporarily skip questions you don't know

COMMENT: Notice that a good understanding of the article can be shown with just the main idea and major details. Furthermore, stating the main idea and major details in your own words will show your basic understanding of the article.

ACTIVITY 4.2

The main idea of the following article is underlined. To practice locating major details, do the following:

- Underline the signal words that indicate major details.
- Write a summary outline that includes the topic, main idea, and major details. Remember to write the outline in your own words to be sure you understand the material.

How to Preview a Textbook

One of the most helpful things you can do when you begin a new class in college is to preview your textbook. To do this follow these simple steps:

First, examine the table of contents. This will quickly tell you how many chapters are in the book and the nature of the material covered. Second, read the "To the Student" section or the Preface, if there is one, to see how the book is organized and how the author approaches the material. Among other things, this will tell you if the book is practical or theoretical in approach. Then examine the copyright date to see how recent the text is. This could be important. If you want recent information on medicine or world geography, for example, you do not want a very old book. Finally, check to see what special features the book contains. For example, is there an index at the back listing important terms and concepts? Is there a glossary where terms are defined? Is the book arranged chapter-by-chapter or alphabetically? Is there an appendix of additional information? Are there summaries at the end of each chapter? By taking just a few minutes to preview your next textbook, you can get more out of your book in a shorter amount of time.

Key Sentences

An author does not always write signal words before major details. When there are few or no signal words, you must look for key sentences that contain reasons, causes, effects, examples, or steps of a process. Ask yourself, "Which sentences in the article make the main idea understandable or believable?"

MODEL 4.3: Locating Major Details Without the Aid of Signal Words

Read the following article and notice the major details that are in italics. The first sentence is underlined because it is the main idea.

Test Anxiety

Whenever I take a test I get nervous, and it shows. I can't help it. *My hands shake so much I can hardly hold my pen.* I'm sure everyone notices, but I can't control it. They must think I have some disease of the muscles, but it only happens at test time. *The palms of my hands get sweaty, and I have to keep wiping them on my pants to keep them dry.* Shaky, sweaty hands do not write good tests.

My stomach tightens up and my head aches. I feel as if I have eaten too much, even when I have an empty stomach. It's very distracting, even painful. If I take a pain reliever for my headache, it often further irritates my stomach. I am just not able to think about the test.

I am working to control my nervousness but have not had much luck. I will keep trying, but I may need to get some help. It is a problem too big for me to tackle alone right now.

COMMENT: Even though no signal words are used to indicate major details, it is clear that the major details describe physical reactions to nervousness about taking tests. The last paragraph is a restatement of the main idea expressing the author's intention to keep working on the problem.

ACTIVITY 4.3

Read the following article. Underline the main idea of the article and any signal words that indicate major details. Then write a summary outline listing the **topic, main idea,** and **major details.** Do not include signal words in your summary outline.

Why Take Good Notes?

Perhaps you have been told to take good notes in order to get better grades. "Oh sure," you think, "it might help, but it's a lot of work. It may not be worth the effort." Actually, taking good class notes is important for several reasons.

For one thing, note-taking helps you keep your mind on what the instructor is saying. If you are trying to write the important ideas of the lecture, you have to keep your mind focused. We all know how easy it is to let our minds wander during some classes.

Second, notes are a good memory aid. They remind you of future assignments and due dates, and they provide you with review sheets before tests. Most of us do not have photographic memories, but good notes can remind us of the classroom experience.

Sometimes an instructor lectures on the same ideas as those in your textbook. Often the textbooks are long and difficult to read. Good notes can help clarify material in the textbook when your instructor covers ideas from the book. It is important to get the necessary information, but it usually does not matter where you get it.

Last, good notes are a record of information that might not be included in your textbook, but which your instructor expects you to know. Often, instructors test primarily on class lectures, even when a textbook is assigned. You will find that, with very few exceptions, good class notes are more than worth all the effort it takes to produce them. The rewards are called good grades and pride in your accomplishment.

ACTIVITY 4.4

Read the following article. Underline the main idea and any signal words that indicate major details. Then write an outline listing the **topic, main idea,** and **major details.**

How to Take Good Notes

When you are convinced that good note-taking is important to your success in school, you might want to learn some of the important steps in the process. Often, no one has taught you how to take good notes, yet teachers have expected you to do this since you have been in school. It's important to find the style that works for you, but several steps are involved in almost all good note-taking systems.

The first step is to date and label your notes. This is simple and quick, but it is important. It keeps your notes organized. If an instructor says you will be tested on the material from the two previous weeks, which covers the human skeleton, you will be able to quickly identify what to study.

Next, consider how your notes look. Two things are important here. Leave plenty of space as you take notes. This allows you to fill in words or ideas you may have missed and still keep your notes neat and readable. Furthermore, you should devise a method for indicating key points. Some people underline these points; others put a star or check beside them; still others indicate them by indenting either the major points or the sub-points. The important thing is not *how* you identify them, but that you *do* identify them.

Be sure you always take notes in your own words. To do this, develop your own shorthand or system of abbreviations so that you can concentrate on listening rather than on writing. Putting ideas in your own words, even in abbreviations, is the only way to be sure you understand the material.

Perhaps the most important step is to get in the habit of editing your notes soon after class. By doing this you will automatically review the important ideas from class, fill in any information you wrote down in sketchy form, and realize what you missed so that you can ask questions later. Try to review notes within twenty-four hours after class.

Strategies for Understanding Longer Articles

So far the articles in the models and exercises in this chapter have been rather short. Most articles you will read are much longer, and identifying the main idea and major details usually becomes a greater challenge due to the increased length. Like any other skill, however, the ability to find major details improves with practice. Here are some suggestions to help you develop this skill

1. Follow *all* of the preview steps discussed in Chapter Three:
   - read the title
   - look at pictures, subtitles, and headings
   - read the first and last paragraphs
   - read the first sentence of each of the other paragraphs
   - read any questions that follow the article
2. Divide the article into sections that indicate the introduction, main idea, major details, and conclusion. Sections may consist of one or more paragraphs. Check the main idea of each paragraph to see if it is a major detail of the article. Do not assume that each paragraph contains a major detail.
3. Label each section of the article in the margin of the book.

MODEL 4.4: Locating Major Details in an Article

Read this article and notice how it is divided into sections. Then look at the sample summary outline that follows the article.

The Importance of Childhood Memories

by Norman M. Lobsenz
from *Reader's Digest*

***Section One:* Introduction**

Some years ago, when my young wife became desperately ill, I wondered how I would be able to cope with the physical and emotional burden of caring for her. One night, when I was drained of strength and endurance, a long-forgotten incident came to mind.

I was about ten years old at the time and my mother was seriously ill. I had gotten up in the middle of the night to get a drink of water. As I passed my parents' bedroom, I saw the light on. I looked inside. My father was sitting in a chair in his bathrobe next to Mother's bed, doing nothing. She was asleep. I rushed into the room.

"What's wrong?" I cried. "Why aren't you asleep?"

Dad soothed me. "Nothing's wrong. I'm just watching over her."

I can't say exactly how, but the memory of that long-ago incident gave me the strength to take up my own burden again. The remembered light and warmth from my parents' room were curiously powerful and my father's words haunted me: "I'm just watching over her." The role I now assumed seemed somehow more bearable, as if a resource [had] been called from the past or from within.

***Section Two:* Main Idea**

In moments of psychological jeopardy, such memories often turn out to be the ultimate resources of personality, dark prisms which focus our basic feeling about life. As Sir James Barrie once wrote, "God gives us memory so that we may have roses in December."

***Section Three:* Major Detail**
(Can't predict what makes lasting memories.)

No parent can ever really know which memory, planted in childhood, will grow to be a rose. Often our most vivid and enduring remembrances are of apparently simple, even trivial things. I did not discover this myself until one bright, leaf-budding spring day when my son Jim and I were putting a fresh coat of paint on the porch railing. We were talking about plans to celebrate his approaching 15th birthday, and I found myself thinking how quickly his childhood had passed.

"What do you remember best?" I asked him.

He answered without a moment's hesitation.

"The night we were driving somewhere, just you and me, on a dark road, and you stopped the car and helped me catch fireflies."

Fireflies? I could have thought of a dozen incidents, both pleasant and unpleasant, that might have remained vivid in his mind. But fireflies? I searched my memory—and eventually it came back to me.

I'd been driving cross-country, traveling late to meet a rather tight schedule. I had stopped to clean the windshield, when all at once a cloud of fireflies surrounded us. Jim, who was five years old then, was tremendously excited. He wanted to catch one. I was tired and tense, and anxious to get on to our destination. I was about to tell him that we didn't have time to waste when something changed my mind. In the trunk of the car I found an empty glass jar. Into it we scooped dozens of the insects. And while Jim watched them glow, I told him of the mysterious cold light they carried in their bodies. Finally, we uncapped the jar and let the fireflies blink away into the night.

"Why do you remember that?" I asked. "It doesn't seem terribly important."

> "I don't know," he said. "I didn't even know I did remember it until just now." Then a few moments later: "Maybe I do know why. Maybe it was because I didn't think you were going to stop and catch any with me—and you did."

Since that day I have asked many friends to reach back into their childhoods and tell me what they recall with greatest clarity. Almost always they mention similar moments—experiences or incidents not of any great importance. Not crises or trauma or triumphs, but things which, although small in themselves, carry sharp sensations of warmth and joy, or sometimes pain.

One friend I spoke with was the son of an executive who was often away from home. "Do you know what I remember best?" he said to me. "It was the day of the annual school picnic, when my usually very dignified father appeared in his shirt-sleeves, sat on the grass with me, ate a box lunch, and then made the longest hit in our softball game. I found out later that he [had] postponed a business trip to Europe to be there." My friend is a man who experiences the world as a busy, serious place but who basically feels all right about it and about himself. His favorite childhood memory is both clue to and cause of his fundamental soundness.

***Section Four:* Major Detail** *(Parents can help shape memories.)*

Clearly, the power parents have to shape the memories of their children involves an awesome responsibility. In this respect nothing is trivial. What to a grownup might seem a casual word or action often is, to a child, the kernel of a significant memory on which he will build. As grownups, we draw on these memories as sources of strength or weakness. Author Willa Cather saw this clearly. "There are those early memories," she wrote. "One cannot get another set; one has only those."

Not long ago, I talked with a woman who has married a young and struggling sculptor. She cheerfully accepted their temporary poverty. "I grew up during the depression," she said. "My dad scrambled from one job to another. But I remembered that each time a job ended, my mother would scrape together enough money to make us an especially good dinner. She used to call them our 'trouble meals.' I know now that they were her way of showing Dad she believed in him, in his ability to fight back. I learned that loving someone is more important than having something."

Section Five:
Major Detail
(Steps to provide good memories.)

If childhood memories are so important, what can parents do to help supply their children with a healthy set?

❑ For one thing, parents should be aware of the memory-building process. In our adult preoccupation, we tend to think that the "important" experiences our children will have are still in their future. We forget that, to them, childhood is reality rather than merely a preparation for reality. We forget that childhood memories form the adult personality. "What we describe as 'character,'" wrote Sigmund Freud, "is based on the memory traces of our earliest youth."

❑ Parents can try to find the extra energy, time, or enthusiasm to carry out the small and "insignificant" plan that is so important to a child. The simple act of baking that special batch of cookies or helping to build that model car, even though you are tired or harried, may make an important memory for your youngster.

Conversely, parents can try to guard against the casual disillusionments and needless disappointments which they often unthinkingly inflict on children. I would venture that almost everyone has a memory of an outing canceled or a promise broken without a reason or an explanation. "My father always used to say, 'We'll see,'" one man told me. "I soon learned that what that meant was 'no,' but without any definite reason."

Parents can think back to their own childhoods and call up their own memories. By remembering the incidents that made important impressions on them, parents can find guideposts to ways in which they can shape the future memories of their own youngsters.

Finally, parents can, by their own actions and words, communicate emotions as well as experiences to their children. We can give them a memory of courage rather than fear; of strength rather than weakness; of an appetite for adventure rather than a shrinking from new people and places; of warmth and affection rather than rigidity and coldness. In just such memories are rooted the attitudes and feeling that characterize a person's entire approach to life.

Sample Summary Outline

What is the article about? (**Topic**)

Why childhood memories are important

What is the author's main point about the topic? (**Main Idea**)

Childhood memories can help us get through tough times.

Or you might write,

In tough times, childhood memories can give us strength.

How does the author support the main idea? (**Major Details**)

Parents can't predict what makes lasting memories.

Parents can help shape their children's memories in four ways:

1. *be aware of the importance of memory process*
2. *try to find extra time and energy for children's activities*
3. *recall your own childhood memories*
4. *share both your emotions and experiences with children*

COMMENT: Notice that not every paragraph contains a major detail. For example, Section One (the introduction) is five paragraphs long and Section Three (one long example) is nine paragraphs long.

ACTIVITY 4.5

Read the following article and complete all of the steps you have learned so far. Preview the article, divide it into sections, and label the sections. Then write a summary outline stating the topic, main idea, and major details.

Listen Carefully

by Tom W. Harris

Consultant Germaine Knapp wants you to hear something. "Effective listening—we call it power listening—is one of the strongest assets in professional life today," she says. "Too few of us take advantage of it, but all of us could. There are dozens of field-proven techniques and tactics for applying the power of listening, and they get results."

Knapp is president of Wordsmart Inc., a consulting and training firm in Rochester, NY. Her clients include Xerox and Eastman Kodak as well as banks, hospitals, manufacturers, and colleges. Training in listening skills is one of Knapp's specialties.

Knapp cites observations by Lyman K. Steil, a former University of Minnesota professor who is president of Communication Development Inc., a consulting firm in St. Paul, MN. He has developed and carried out programs designed to improve employees' listening skills. His programs have ranged from a multimillion-dollar, listening-oriented advertising campaign some years ago for Sperry Corp.—now Unisys—to training for countless small and midsized enterprises.

"Overall," Steil says, "if each of America's more than 100 million workers prevented just one $10 mistake by better listening, their organizations would gain over $1 billion in profits. A $10 mistake is as simple as a few minutes' error in the time of a meeting, putting an item of stock in the wrong place, or having to retype a letter."

Knapp says that effective listening—or power listening—can be used to help persuade, motivate, improve productivity, boost morale, obtain cooperation, sell, teach, inform, or achieve other goals. "Effective listening is continually active, not passive," she says. "For example, to draw out information from the other person and get the whole story, actively show that you're listening. We train people in a number of techniques that are very simple—and very effective," such as gestures and comments.

Gestures and mannerisms can communicate interest. Lean forward rather than back while listening, Knapp suggests. Nod occasionally to show comprehension. Smile. Look directly at the person speaking. Comments such as "I see" and "Go on" can show that you are attuned to what the speaker is saying. When used with sincerity, these tactics can pay dividends.

Another way to improve listening is to take notes, Knapp says. "It helps make you focus on the highlights of what's being said. And the other person, seeing you write things down, will usually try to maximize accuracy and clarity. One word of caution: Too much note-taking may make some people angry or nervous and uncommunicative."

Consultant Steil has found that note taking also works in phone conversations. He cites the example of a salesman who habitually made comments such as, "Just a second—could you mention that again—I want to write it down." In the salesman's view, "better listening made better sales." Customers became more precise in explaining their needs, he said, and they were favorably impressed with his diligence for detail.

Business people in various fields have adopted effective-listening tactics. For example, Dan Fazenden, president of Roger Fazenden Realty Inc., a real estate company near Minneapolis, says: "I use the 'plan to report' principle. When someone tells you something, listen so intently that you could report it all to someone else."

It is important to "listen for what isn't said," Knapp says, as well as to ask questions. She stresses two important rules:

"Never end a conversation without being sure what was said—and why. Furthermore, don't pretend you understand when you don't. Chances are the speaker, not you, caused the confusion. So don't walk away and later make mistakes that you, not the speaker, will be held responsible for."

Once your employees become good listeners, it will pay you in turn to listen to those listeners, says auto dealer John Zimbrick of Madison, WI. Zimbrick's employees listen to customers to determine their attitudes, and management keeps current on the employees' findings. "It can be even more effective than customer-research projects," says Zimbrick. "Many firms can't afford specialized customer research. This can do the job better."

The other side of power listening is the power to make other people listen. Knapp explains: "One of the most skillful communicators I know of has an office position in a medium-sized business. When she senses somebody isn't listening, she stops talking. She lets two or three seconds tick away. The other person 'hears' this pause and gets back to listening." Other effective tactics, she says, include leaning forward, standing up, gesturing, asking a question.

For a typical employee, Knapp says, time spent communicating during the workday may be as high as 50 percent, and for top managers, the figure can reach 75 percent. "An average 45 percent of this time is spent listening," she says. "So, either for an individual or an organization, when you polish up listening skills, you may well be tapping into your greatest undeveloped success resources."

ACTIVITY 4.6

Read the following article and complete all of the steps you have learned so far. Preview the article, divide it into sections, and label the sections. Then write a summary outline stating the topic, main idea, and major details.

You and Public Speaking

by Andrew Wolvin, Roy M. Berko, and Darlyn R. Wolvin

When you decide to register for a course in public speaking, you may think, "I like to get up and speak to audiences, so this class should be no problem." Maybe, though, your thoughts are more in the line of "Me, get up before a class and give a speech? No way!" If that is your response, feel some comfort in realizing that for most of us there is an element of uncertainty, or in some cases out-and-out fear, when it comes to **public speaking**—the act of communication that occurs between one person and an audience.

Some people actually do enjoy speaking before groups. If that were not true we would not have politicians, teachers, media performers, and religious leaders. On the other hand, research shows that 61 percent of the people in the United States are afraid of giving speeches.

One of the purposes of a speech course, is to teach you the skills necessary to prepare and present an effective speech or to reinforce the skills you already have. People who are confident of their public speaking abilities naturally have more positive attitudes about communicating to an audience than those who lack these skills.

A study aptly titled "Do Real People Ever Give Speeches?" revealed that, although many of us try to avoid public speaking, people at all levels do indeed give presentations. In fact, 55 percent of the respondents gave at least one speech to 10 or more people every two years; 71 percent of these speakers gave at least four speeches during that time. People with more education and income give speeches more frequently. Knowing this, a person who wants a high-income job is wise to get a solid education and prepare to become an effective speaker. And it is not only the business world which requires public speaking. Your participation in a class, club, volunteer activity, or political situation may call on your public communication skills.

No matter what your career choice, most college graduates enter occupations that require some form of speaking before groups, whether within the organization, at conferences or conventions, or as a representative of the company. Businesses are acutely aware of this requirement. A survey of Fortune 500 companies revealed that presentation skills were identified as "somewhat important" for secretarial staff and hourly wage workers; "important" for supervisors and technical staff; and "very important" for sales staff, executives, middle managers, and human resource staff. Eighty-two percent of the Fortune 500 companies responding to this survey indicated that presentation skills are so important that they provide speech training in order to increase employee performance.

Public speaking occurs both within the organization to groups of employees and to various groups outside, such as potential customers. Because communication is so central to productivity and effectiveness, many organizations offer public speaking training for their employees. One such company with an intricate communication plan is Honeywell. Honeywell's corporate communication department has established a speakers' bureau with a specific public communication objective: to identify appropriate speaking platforms, negotiate media interviews, publish speakers' remarks, and provide opportunities to reach customers and prospects.

Interest in effective public communication also is reflected in the growth of speakers' agents, who book speakers for the annual sales meetings, conventions, and other large meetings that companies and organizations often sponsor. A former chief executive officer of Chrysler Corporation stresses that public speaking is "the best way to motivate a large group." The speaking industry is lucrative. Well-known celebrities can command $25,000 or more for a speech.

Skill in public speaking also is important in the academic arena. Students are asked to do classroom presentations of research projects, reports, experiments, and studies. Outside of class you might give a report to a student organization, make a proposal to your fraternity or sorority, represent a political candidate, or give a speech as part of a job interview.

Public communication is the lifeblood of political, legal, advertising, and promotional work. But you do not have to work in one of the media professions to be pressed into delivering a message effectively. During Operation Desert Storm, a military leader served as a highly effective communicator. The world was riveted to the television screen for regular briefings by General Norman Schwarzkopf, com-mander of the U.S. forces in the Persian Gulf. It was clear how much public speaking skills can accomplish. Schwarzkopf's success, though resounding, was not unique.

Public speaking has a long and colorful history. Being aware of this tradition allows us to realize that public speaking customs and processes are based on many trials and errors, theories, imitations of great speakers, and research into effective speaking.

Rate Your Presenting Skills

Labeling each of these statements as true or false will tell you if you know what it takes to be a powerful presenter:

1. Visuals will keep the audience's attention better if you use a variety of type fonts and sizes.
2. Memorizing a speech isn't a good idea.
3. Each visual should include no more then two key concepts.
4. Casually leaning back on one hip tells an audience that you're less formal and thus more believable.
5. To get an audience to think creatively, project information on the right side of a screen.

Answers: **1.** False. Audiences react better to consistency, so use no more than one or two fonts. Also, it's best to use a sans seri font because it's easier to read in the larger sizes you need for the screen. **2.** True, but some experts recommend that you memorize the first minute or two to help build confidence by starting strong. **3.** False. Limit each visual to only one key concept or risk confusing an audience with too much to recall at once. **4.** False. It signals—nonverbally—that you wish you didn't have to be there. **5.** True. Research also shows that you should put the image or the words as high on the screen as you can get them.

Source: *Communication Briefing*, February 1998.

Excerpted and adapted from: Andrew Wolvin, Roy M. Berko, and Darlyn R. Wolvin, *The Public Speaker/The Public Listener*, pp. 3–4.

Self-Check Review

1. How do signal words help you to find major details?
2. How do you locate major details if there are no signal words?
3. Why is it important to locate major details?
4. How can you use the information in this chapter in school, at work, and in your personal life? ✦

Chapter Five

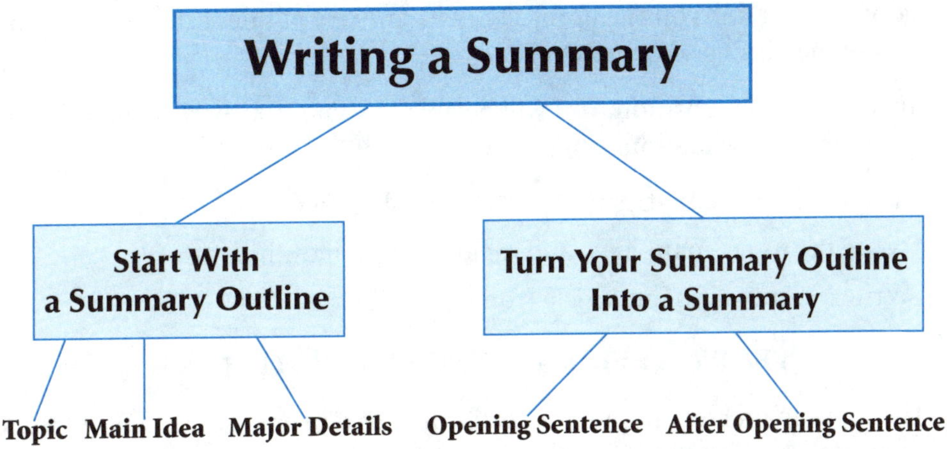

When you write a summary of an article, you rewrite what someone else has written. You write a shorter version, using your own words and sentence style. To write a shorter version of an article, you focus on the author's main idea and major details.

Knowing how to write a good summary can benefit you in school in several ways:

1. A written summary allows you to measure your understanding of an article because you have to write it in your own words.
2. You can improve your grades because many college courses require written summaries.
3. You can write better term papers because such assignments require you to summarize long articles and books before you write your paper.

Benefits can also be found in the workplace:

1. You often have an increased chance of getting a job because of writing skills shown on your application, some of which ask you to summarize your employment history.
2. You can keep your good standing in a company or get promoted by displaying good writing skills on such projects as a summary of sales activity, or summaries of meetings and conferences.
3. In a managerial position, you will be able to write summaries in the form of performance evaluations of employees.

The models and activities in this chapter will help you to

- Write the topic, main idea, and major details in outline form.
- Write a summary of an article from an outline.

Start With a Summary Outline

The topic, main idea, and major details of an article are the elements of a good summary outline. You identified the topic and main idea of an article in Chapter Three, and you located major details in Chapter Four. When you put these elements together, you have a summary outline from which you can write a good summary.

Your summary outline should include the following:

- the topic (stated in a word or phrase)
- the main idea (stated in a complete sentence)
- a list of major details (stated in phrases or sentences)

MODEL 5.1: The Summary Outline of an Article

Below is an article you read in Chapter Four. A summary outline of the article is modeled for you.

How to Preview a Textbook

One of the most helpful things you can do when you begin a new class in college is to preview your textbook. To do this, follow these simple steps. First, examine the table of contents. This will quickly tell you how many chapters are in the book and the nature of the material covered. Second, read the "To the Student" section or the Preface, if there is one, to see how the book is organized and how the author approaches the material. Among other things, this will tell you if the book is practical or theoretical in approach. Then examine the copyright date to see how recent the text is. Finally, check to see what special features the book contains. For example, check to see if there is an Index at the back listing important terms and concepts. Is there a Glossary where terms are defined? Is the book arranged chapter-by-chapter or alphabetically? Is there an appendix of additional information? Locate summaries at the end of each chapter. By taking just a few minutes to preview your next textbook, you can get more out of your book in a shorter amount of time.

What is the paragraph about? (**Topic**)

How to preview a textbook

Or you might write,

Previewing a textbook

What is the author's main point about the topic? (**Main Idea**)

Previewing a textbook is helpful and it involves just four steps.

How does the author support the topic? (**Major Details**)

Look at table of contents
Read any introductory material
Check copyright date
Look for special features, such as a glossary, appendix, and summaries

Turn Your Summary Outline Into a Summary

Your outline can be turned into a summary in three steps:

1. Write an opening sentence.
2. Change phrases of the outline into complete sentences.
3. Add necessary information.

Writing the Opening Sentence

The opening sentence of a summary should contain the article's title and author, if given, as well as the author's main idea.

Here are sample opening sentences for articles you read in previous chapters of this book:

A. Everlasting love is a dangerous illusion according to Scott Peck in "The Myth of Romantic Love."

OR

Scott Peck, in "The Myth of Romantic Love," warns us that the idea of everlasting love is an illusion.

B. In "The Importance of Childhood Memories," Norman M. Lobsenz describes how childhood memories can help us get through difficult times.

C. In "Test Anxiety," the author describes the physical symptoms experienced before taking a test.

Notice that the verbs in each of these examples are written in present tense. Here are some other verbs you might use for these opening sentences:

Scott Peck *explains* . . .

Norman Lobsenz *states* . . .

The author *relates* . . .

Later in the summary, you may wish to use the author's name again. Once you have given the full name, use only the author's last name throughout your summary.

Peck also lists . . .

Lobsenz further examines . . .

After the Opening Sentence

- A good summary contains major details of the article.
- A good summary contains any explanation necessary to clarify the major details.
- A good summary is written primarily in your own words. If you use more than three consecutive words from the article, use quotation marks. Occasionally

you might quote an important phrase or sentence, but your summary should never be simply a string of quotations.

- The length of a summary varies. However, a good summary is usually no longer than one-fourth the length of the article you are summarizing.

MODEL 5.2: Summary Outline and Summary of an Article

Following this article is a model of a summary outline and a summary of the article.

Child Abuse: Can It Rewire the Brain?

from *Parenting Exchange*
by Joy Goss and Maria Fisicaro

A review of 166 studies from 1985 to 1997 (*JAMA* Dec 2, 1998) concludes that up to 20 percent of boys had been sexually abused. What were the long-term consequences? One third of juvenile delinquents, 40 percent of sexual offenders, and 76 percent of serial rapists reported they were sexually abused as teenagers. Can abuse at an early age rewire the brain? Can exposure to domestic violence and neglect damage brain circuits?

High-resolution brain imaging techniques and advancing knowledge of neurochemistry suggest violence is the result of environment and biology, sometimes exclusively or sometimes one complementing the other. Genetics, brain structure, and environment all play an important role in the induction of this aberrant behavior.

Accumulating evidence shows that early childhood trauma and/or specific damage to the brain explains why one person acts more impulsively, and often more violently, than the average population. Although genetic endowment plays in the development of the brain, human development is primarily shaped by prenatal and early childhood care. External stimulation—sounds the child hears (parents fighting), touches the child feels (prenatal and child abuse), and the world the child sees (environment)—influences the way the child's brain is formed. In babies repeatedly and roughly shaken, the white fibers that link the prefrontal cortex with other brain structures can be lacerated, effectively cutting off the rest of the brain from prefrontal regulatory control. When the prefrontal cortex, which regulates behaviors, is damaged, it predisposes an individual to violence.

People who come from violent environments are more likely to use violence as a coping method; violent people who grew up in normal, healthy environments tend to have been internally influenced by poor brain functioning. There is a strong belief among the experts that when a child is emotionally neglected, abused, or overprotected early in life, capacities for empathy, attachment, and emotional control are impaired, and the individual's emerging unique identity can be thwarted regardless of socio-economic condition, cultural background, or race.

There is no question that child abuse has long-term negative consequences; in the meantime, safe, loving, nurturing foster homes must be found for those children who have been abused or neglected by their own families. However, continued shrinkage in the number of suitable places and competent adults willing to care for abused children does not augur well for their future.

Reprinted from Joy Goss and Maria Fisicaro, "Child Abuse: Can It Rewire the Brain?" *Parenting Exchange*, May/June 2001, Vol. 4, Number 5, page 6. Reprinted by permission,

Outline

What is the article about? (**Topic**)

The effects of childhood abuse

What is the author's main point about the topic? (**Main Idea**)

Abuse can damage a child's brain circuits, producing long-term negative behavior.

How does the author support the main idea? (**Major Details**)

- *Studies show that a high proportion of dysfunctional adult males were abused as children*
- *Modern technology reveals that brain damage accounts for some violent behavior*
- *Abusive acts (violent sounds and actions) can damage the brain*
- *Impairment due to abuse cuts across cultural, economic, and racial lines*
- *More good foster homes and caregivers are needed; both are declining in numbers*

Summary

In "Child Abuse: Can It Rewire the Brain?" Joy Goss and Maria Fisicaro report that abuse at an early age can affect brain function and produce long-term negative effects. They note that a disproportionately high number of adult males who are sexual offenders were abused as children. In fact, 76 percent of serial rapists report being abused. Furthermore, modern science has shown that both genetics and environment play a role in abnormal behavior.

Goss and Fisicaro explain that sights, sounds, and touches, all environmental factors, can damage fibers in the brain. A young person's brain is quite fragile. The prefrontal cortex is the part of the brain that regulates behaviors; when shaking or other violent behaviors damage this part of a child's brain, he or she is more prone to violence. The authors conclude that abused children need the safe, loving environment of good foster homes. However, both foster homes and those who work in them are shrinking in number, so the outlook is not bright.

COMMENT: The first sentence of the summary identifies the authors, the title of the article, and the main idea. The title contains a question, and the second paragraph of the article repeats the question and adds a related question. Remember that the main idea statement cannot be stated in the form of a question; however, the answer to a question posed in a title, or early on in an essay, is often the main idea.

ACTIVITY 5.1

Read the article below. An outline is provided. Write a summary from the outline, using one of the main idea sentences provided for you in the model outline.

Repairing Your Car

Good mechanics can save you a lot of money during the lifetime of your car. More important, they can save your life. Since good mechanics are so important to car owners, it is helpful to know where to find them. Good mechanics may be found working in a variety of places.

Dealers' service departments specialize in repairs of particular makes of cars, and their mechanics are given special training by the manufacturer. They are the highest paid in the industry. You would be wise to use your dealer while your warranty is in effect.

Independent garages can and often do charge less than a dealer due to lower overhead. Their reliability is largely dependent on the individual in charge. It is a good idea to check out a garage's reputation by questioning local residents and customers if possible.

Specialty shops service one part of the car only: radiators, tires, mufflers, automatic transmissions, ignitions, or brakes. Usually these mechanics are very skilled within their areas of expertise.

Service departments of chain department and discount stores are usually located near large shopping areas. Their mechanics are experienced in making fast, relatively simple repairs and replacements, particularly on popular U.S. cars—but they probably lack training and experience to diagnose complex mechanical problems.

Gasoline stations offer the advantages of a close-in location and conveniently long hours. In addition, their owners are not likely to take advantage of good, regular customers. For routine maintenance and minor repair jobs, you would probably find a neighborhood service station satisfactory.

Automotive diagnostic centers possess highly sophisticated electronic equipment to evaluate the various mechanical systems of a car, diagnose existing problems, and predict future ones. Authentic diagnostic centers are usually not in the repair business themselves. Charges are quite low.

Outline

What is the article about? (**Topic**)

Places to take your car for repair

What is the author's main point about the topic? (**Main Idea**)

You can find a good mechanic at a number of places.

Or you might write,
There are a number of good places to take your car for repair.

How does the author support the main idea? (**Major Details**)

Dealer service departments good for warranty work
Independent garages charge less but should be checked
Specialty shops for just one type of repair
Discount or department stores convenient for minor repairs
Gas stations open long hours—best for routine work
Some automotive centers for diagnosing only

COMMENT: Notice that details about each of these locations are provided. These details are important; a list of repair places without this information would neither help you understand the article nor summarize it.

ACTIVITY 5.2

Complete these steps for the following two articles.

1. Preview the article.
2. Read the article.
3. Divide the article into sections and label the sections.
4. Outline the article, including the topic, main idea, and major details.
5. Write a summary of the article from your summary outline.

Wool . . . The Living Fiber

by Joseph Plaidly
from Pendleton Woolen Mills pamphlet

For centuries man has gratefully accepted the protective qualities of wool. By the careful crossbreeding of sheep, he has developed fibers of different lengths, diameters, and various degrees of softness and crispness.

Wool is almost custom-made by nature to fit the needs of man. In its processing and manufacture, man takes up where sheep left off. But while new processes and treatments have made wool more versatile in its uses, man has not improved the fiber itself. Wool has a number of characteristics that make it an ideal material.

Wool is the only fiber possessing a natural crimp, or wave. It is the crimp which gives wool its resiliency and vitality. Wool can be stretched to 50 percent of its length and returned to its original dimension without damage. It can be twisted out of shape and subjected to repeated strain under dry or wet conditions. The crimps will always return to their original positions.

The outer scaly covering of wool sheds water, making it naturally rain resistant. The protein cortex, on the contrary, readily absorbs moisture. Like a sponge, wool can absorb up to 30 percent of its weight in water or body vapor without becoming damp. This quality also enables woolen clothing to absorb normal perspiration.

Wool provides the most warmth with the least weight. This is due to the millions of air spaces enclosed within its compression-resistant structure. In clothing, wool acts as a shield against cold and hot air. It regulates the loss or gain of heat and keeps the body at its normal temperature.

Wool is the most naturally wrinkle-resistant of all fibers. Its spindle-shaped molecules have an affinity for one another and a determination to remain folded together in their normal arrangement. Wrinkles caused by body movements during wear or compression in a suitcase displace and stretch the material. When the wool relaxes, it corrects any displacement and returns to its original position, eliminating the wrinkle.

Wool takes dye completely, permanently, and beautifully. Striking evidence can be observed in the dye kettles. When wool is dyed, the dye in the liquid agent is completely absorbed, leaving behind only a clear solution in the kettles after the wool is removed.

Wool resists fading from sunlight, atmospheric impurities, and perspiration. It maintains its natural luster for years of service and wear. Even after wool has been worn for many years, it can be shredded back into fiber to be spun and woven into new fabrics. The recovery and re-use of wool in low-price fabrics is an industry of its own.

Wool is also nonflammable. Fire insurance companies recommend the use of wool blankets, rugs, or coats to extinguish flames. Practically all laboratory or industrial activity involving highly flammable materials requires that wool blankets be made available to extinguish small fires or ignited clothing. Wool, unless it is in continued direct contact with flame, will extinguish any fire. The denser the weave and the greater the weight of a wool fabric, the less likely it is even to char due to its low-oxygen content.

Another property of wool is its lack of static. Static attracts dirt from the air and imbeds it in fabrics. This quality makes wool the easiest of all fabrics to keep clean. Freedom from static permits woolen fabrics to hang and drape in natural lines, unlike materials woven from artificial fabrics or blends.

Finally, wool is a living fiber, intricate in its chemical composition and physical structure. It is composed of cells that grow out of the inner follicles in the skin of sheep. Wool forms within the protection of a wax-like substance called *wool grease,* which protects the fibers as the sheep forages for food. The fiber also contains suint, the salts of perspiration. In the first step of processing, the wool grease, or suint, and other foreign matter adhering to the fiber, are removed. Refinement of the wool grease produces lanolin, the base of beauty preparations and the perfect carrier for medicinal ointments. The lanolin and its by-products are also used as a rust preventive.

Patricia Fripp, Professional Motivational Speaker

"Come out punching!" Counsel from an enthusiastic boxing trainer? No, this is sound public speaking advice from Patricia Fripp, a popular motivational speaker. Although her information brochures quietly promote her as "A Speaker for All Reasons," she has been hailed as "electrifying," "highly energetic," and "a forceful presence."

In 1966, at age 20, Fripp left her native England and set foot in the United States armed only with a positive attitude, $500, and her skill as a hair stylist. She had no job, nowhere to live, and no contacts. But, she says wryly, she "knew everyone in America was rich, and movie stars flocked through the streets!" Fripp worked as a hair stylist in San Francisco and eventually began traveling as a demonstrator of various beauty products and techniques. Because her stories and chats about her business experience added noticeable flair to her demonstrations, audience members soon began inviting her to speak at their Rotary Clubs, Kiwanis Clubs, and other civic organizations.

In 1977 Fripp attended her first National Speakers' Association Convention. Seven years later, she became the National Speakers' Association's first woman president. She is a Certified Speaking Professional (CSP) and has received the Council of Peers Award of Excellence (CPAE), the highest recognition for professionalism in speaking. In general, her work ranges from 25-minute keynote speeches to all-day seminars. She has spoken to government agencies, at independent rallies, and at meetings for such corporate giants as IBM, AT&T, and General Electric. Her presentations have titles such as "Creative Thinking for Better Business" and "Adapting to Change." Fripp states that her job is to present a message that is "in harmony with, and reflects the philosophy of" the company or organization that hires her.

Fripp's list of "Basic Speaking for Your First or Fifteenth Talk" includes 21 noteworthy recommendations, such as:

> Come out punching! Because people tend to remember a speech's beginning and end, make them worth remembering. Use startling statements or other attention grabbers rather than saying "Good evening ladies and gentlemen. It's a pleasure to be here."

> Recognize that because television has shaped today's audiences, they demand more powerful speakers and have shorter attention spans. Be unique and interesting.
>
> People do not remember what you say as much as what they "see." Tell stories to illustrate your points and make them come alive. A story or vignette should be able to stand alone as a short talk.

Public speaking skill is important for almost all of us. "Your value in the marketplace depends very much upon how easy or difficult it is to replace you," Fripp says. "If you can learn to stand up and speak eloquently with confidence, you will be head and shoulders above your competition." The self-motivated young woman who arrived from England took her own advice and has forged a successful career for herself in the business of motivating others.

Reprinted from: Andrew Wolvin, Roy M. Berko, and Darlyn R. Wolvin, *The Public Speaker/The Public Listener,* p. 165.

ACTIVITY 5.3

In Chapter Four you read two articles and wrote a summary outline of each (Activity 4.5 and Activity 4.6). Now use your outlines to write good summaries of those articles.

Self-Check Review

1. What are the parts of a summary outline?
2. What information is in the opening sentence of a summary?
3. What are the steps in writing a summary?
4. What are some reasons for learning how to write a good summary?
5. How can you use the information in this chapter in school, at work, and in your personal life? ✦

Chapter Six

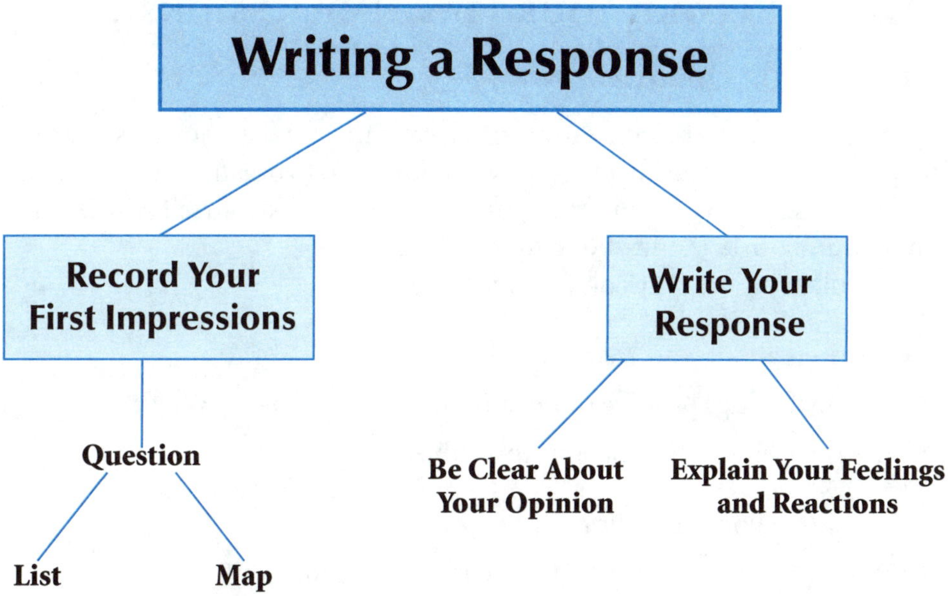

A response is an answer or reply. When you talk with others, you usually reply to their ideas in some fashion. Similarly, as an *active* reader, you respond to the author's ideas by asking questions or perhaps agreeing or disagreeing. The author probably will not hear or read your response, but there is still some interaction between you as the reader and the author. In fact, this interaction helps to make reading fun and meaningful.

In order to write a response, good readers record their first impressions of what they have read. Authors might present an opinion that bothers or pleases you, or they might present you with new information. Your response to what you read is personal and unique and will be influenced by your education and life experiences, cultural heritage, ethnicity, gender, age, and political views.

The models and exercises in this chapter will help you to

- Record your first impressions about an article.
- Write a response to an article.

Record Your First Impressions

The Value of Questioning

Before you write a response to an article, record your first thoughts and feelings. This prewriting or brainstorming activity allows you to organize your thinking before you write. To record your thoughts and feelings, ask yourself a series of questions about the article and about your feelings.

The following are types of questions to ask:

Questions about your *feelings:*

- Are my feelings positive or negative about this subject? Why?
- Are my feelings strong about this subject?

Questions about the *article:*

- What is it about the article that made me feel this way?
- Has the author presented mostly facts or opinions?
- Is the author qualified to write on this subject?
- In what kind of publication was this article printed?
- Do I agree or disagree with the author on the main points?

Questions about *how the author's ideas relate to you:*

- How does the information relate to my own knowledge of the subject?
- How can I use the information I have read?
- Can I add *my* experience and perspective on this subject to help others understand it?

The Process of Listing

Record your initial thoughts and feelings about the ideas you read without worrying about spelling, grammar, or punctuation. List your thoughts as quickly as you can; many times one idea will lead to another, so try to write without stopping.

Answer the preceding questions about your feelings, the article itself, and how the article relates to you. If your answers lead to other thoughts, list those as well. No idea is too unimportant or too silly to list in this first step. Try not to evaluate your responses as you write—just write.

MODEL 6.1: Listing First Impressions

Read "The Myth of Romantic Love" and the first impressions that follow the article. The reactions were written by a student.

The Myth of Romantic Love

by M. Scott Peck, M.D.
from *The Road Less Traveled*

To serve as effectively as it does to trap us into marriage, the experience of falling in love probably must have as one of its characteristics the illusion that the experience will last forever. This illusion is fostered in our culture by the commonly held myth of romantic love, which has its origins in our favorite childhood fairy tales, wherein the prince and the princess, once united, live happily forever after. The myth of romantic love tells us, in effect, that for every young man in the world there is a young woman and only one woman for a man and this has been predetermined "in the stars." When we meet the person for whom we are intended, recognition comes through the fact that we fall in love. We have met the person for whom all the heavens intended us, and since the match is perfect, we will then be able to satisfy all of each other's needs forever and ever, therefore live happily forever after in perfect union and harmony. Should it come to pass, however, that we do not satisfy or meet all of each other's needs and friction arises and we fall out of love, then it is clear that a dreadful mistake was made: We misread the stars; we did not hook up with our one and only perfect match; what we thought was love was not real or "true" love; and nothing can be done about the situation except to live unhappily ever after or get divorced.

While I generally find that great myths are great precisely because they represent and embody great universal truths, the myth of romantic love is a dreadful lie. Perhaps it is a necessary lie in that it ensures the survival of the species by its encouragement and seeming validation of the falling-in-love experience that traps us into marriage. But as a psychiatrist I weep in my heart almost daily for the ghastly confusion and suffering that this myth fosters. Millions of people waste vast amounts of energy desperately and futilely attempting to make the reality of their lives conform to the unreality of the myth. Mrs. A. subjugates herself absurdly to her husband out of a feeling of guilt. "I didn't really love my husband when we married," she says, "I pretended I did. I guess I tricked him into it, so I have no right to complain about him, and I owe it to him to do whatever he wants." Mr. B. laments: "I regret I didn't marry Miss C. I think we could have had a good marriage. But I didn't fall head over heels in love with her, so I assumed she couldn't be the right person for me." Mrs. D., married for two years, becomes severely depressed without apparent cause, and enters therapy stating: "I don't know what's wrong. I've got everything I need, including a perfect marriage." Only months later can she accept the fact that she has fallen out of love with her husband but that this does not mean that she made a horrible mistake. Mr. E., also married two years, begins to suffer intense headaches in the evenings and can't believe they are psychosomatic. "My home life is fine. I love my wife as much as the day I married her. She's everything I ever wanted," he says. But his headaches don't leave him until a year later, when he is able to admit, "She bugs the hell out of me the way she is always wanting, wanting things without regard to my salary," and then able to confront her with her extravagance. Mr. and Mrs. F. acknowledge to each other that they have fallen out of love and then proceed to make each other miserable by mutual rampant infidelity as they each search for the one "true love," not realizing that their very acknowledgement could mark the beginning of the work of their marriage instead of the end.

Even when couples have acknowledged that the honeymoon is over, that they are no longer romantically in love with each other and are able still to be committed to their relationship, they still cling to the myth and attempt to conform their lives to it. "Even though we have fallen out of love, if we act by sheer will power as if we still were in love, then maybe romantic love will return to our lives," their thinking goes. These couples prize togetherness. When they enter couples group therapy (which is the setting in which my wife and I and our close colleagues conduct most serious marriage counseling), they sit together, speak for each other, defend each other's faults and seek to present to the rest of the group a united front, believing this unit to be a sign of the relative health of their marriage and a prerequisite for its improvement. Sooner or later, and usually sooner, we must tell most couples that they are too much married, too closely coupled, and that they need to establish some psychological distance from each other before they can even begin to work constructively on their problems. Sometimes it is actually necessary to physically separate them, directing them to sit apart from each other in the group circle. It is always necessary to ask them to refrain from speaking for each other or defending each other against the group. Over and over again we must say, "Let Mary speak for herself, John," and "John can defend himself, Mary; he's strong enough." Ultimately, if they start in therapy, all couples learn that a true acceptance of their own and each other's individuality and separateness is the only foundation upon which a mature marriage can be based and real love can grow.

List of First Impressions

The student who wrote the following impressions answered the suggested questions about feelings, about the article, and about his relationship to the article. As he answered the questions, a personal experience came to mind, and he ended up writing about this experience in his response.

Feelings

Agree with Peck that most matches are not necessarily made in heaven

This myth is "a dreadful lie"? Not sure I think this romance stuff is that bad

Thoughts about the article

Peck makes it sound like commitment is a fault, resulting from belief in the myth

—couples sometimes ignore true feelings

—I think this is what I did with my ex-girlfriend

Peck is a doctor and sounds like he has worked with a lot of married couples

How this relates to me

I think communication is one of the most important things in a relationship

—by not being honest about falling out of love with my girlfriend, I probably hurt the relationship

—I thought things would get better if I just went along

—could have avoided a terrible fight that ruined our friendship as well as our relationship

The Technique of Mapping

Another way of recording first impressions is called **mapping** or **clustering.** As you can see in Model 6.2, this method is quite different from listing. Mapping shows how ideas relate to each other, and the process helps one idea lead to another. Your personal thoughts and feelings determine the shape of the map. Here is a sample map of the list in Model 6.1.

MODEL 6.2: Mapping First Impressions from an Article

The following map contains the same information that is in the First Impressions List in Model 6.1.

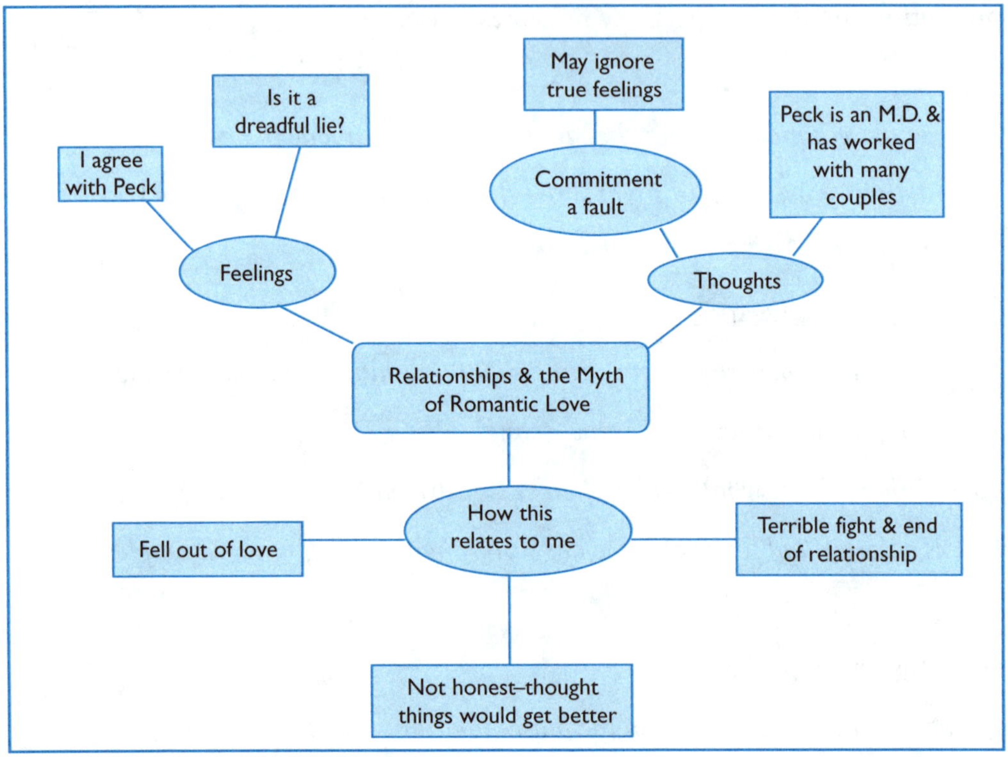

COMMENT: Maps will vary, but here are four suggestions for making and using a map to record your first impressions.

1. Draw a circle or box in the center of a page. Write the subject of the article in the box.
2. Show related ideas in other circles or boxes. Draw lines to show how those ideas are related to the main idea or to each other.
3. Work quickly; don't stop to evaluate your ideas or worry about spelling.
4. When your map is finished, look at it. Is one part more detailed or more interesting to you than the rest? That may be the part you'll want to write about.

ACTIVITY 6.1

Read the following article and write your initial impressions in the form of a list or a map.

Men's Jobs—Women's Jobs

by George Simpson

I heard a woman complain the other day that her new boyfriend never helps her with the laundry and that he'd rather buy new dishes than wash dirty ones. I said, "Sounds like you ought to trade the boyfriend in for a good maid. . . ." I was really thinking, hey, wait a second! It seems to me there's a natural order to life—some things are simply *your* job . . . and some are simply mine. When was the last time you took a whitewall-tire brush to the grill? Or changed the oil in the car? Whose job is it to catch the bat that inadvertently flies in the window? Who *always* puts up the bookshelves? Changes the flat bike tire tubes? Unclogs the gutter?

It's not that I *can't* fold laundry. But you hate it when I don't turn the socks right side out or when I fold the towels into quarters instead of thirds. You have a vision of correctly folded laundry; I do not. It's Nature's way of assigning you that important task. Do you know how to replace the washers in the dripping faucet? I do. That's why it's my job. Seems like part of life's Great Plan.

Don't you agree that there's a pretty good balance between my jobs and yours? And although there's no law that says we can't help each other, let's not make it a skirmish in the battle of the sexes when we don't.

You might counter by saying, "Well, half the laundry is yours." My response: "You ride in the car. But I don't ask you to remember the date of the last tune-up or if it's time to rotate the tires." Because I know that's *my* job. Just like I know it's my job to mow the lawn and shovel the sidewalk.

And it's a good thing men are so compulsive about their jobs. Nobody else would notice that there are only *two* cans of beer left or that we're just about out of garlic-jalapeno-pepper-flavored chips or that the grill needs more propane. Your job, on the other hand, is to keep an eye on the toilet-paper supply and make sure the eggs are thrown out before they hatch.

It's a wonderful balance, don't you think? Isn't it a load off your mind *not* to have to worry about when the gym memberships expire or what time the Redskins game starts on Sunday? Isn't it reassuring to know that you *never* have to worry about cleaning the fish or moving the mulch pile? I know I sleep better not having to think about when the sheets were changed last, how many pints there are in a quart, and the date the new Mel Gibson picture opens. . . .

I don't think that all jobs should be classified as necessarily "women's work" or "a man's job." As a matter of fact, I can out cook and out clean most women I know (and most of them can walk all over me on the tennis court), but we should try to acknowledge the symmetry of having jobs that are ours alone, jobs that if done well—and cheerfully—benefit both of us. And that should be plenty of reward.

ACTIVITY 6.2

If you wrote your first impressions as a list, compare your list with another student's map. If you recorded your first impressions as a map, compare it to someone else's list. Discuss the advantages of each form.

Write Your Response

After you have recorded your initial impressions, the next step is to select one or two ideas from your list or map. Now you can write a response that focuses on the ideas you selected. Here are some guidelines to help you.

Be Clear About Your Opinion

Once you decide on the focus of your response (the topic), write a sentence that states the main point you want to make. In Chapters Three and Four, you practiced identifying authors' main ideas. Now you are the author, stating your main point in what is often called a **topic sentence** or **main idea sentence.**

To write an effective topic sentence, be sure to

- Make a personal connection between what you've read and your own experience. Ask how the information in the article adds to or changes how you act and relate to your surroundings.

- Include a judgment. A response is an opinion, so do not be afraid to clearly state your opinion.

MODEL 6.3: Topic Sentences for a Response

The following are topic sentences students have written for their responses to articles about marriage and relationships.

- *In the articles I read and in my own experience, I realize that relationships are often jeopardized by lack of clear communication.*
- *I do not look at marriage as a step one should take in life in order to be considered successful; however, I do feel that loving marriages are possible.*
- *If a marriage is not based on friendship, it is destined to fail.*

Explain Your Feelings and Thoughts

When responding to an article, you may find that general words such as *interesting, helpful,* or *frightening* are appropriate. However, try to explain how or why you used such a word to describe your feelings. In Chapter Four you identified the major details that authors use to explain or clarify the main idea. As an author, you will want to include examples, facts, and other details to explain your main idea.

It is appropriate to use personal pronouns, such as *I, me, we,* or *us,* in this type of writing.

MODEL 6.4: Response to an Article

The following response was written by the student who wrote the List of First Impressions and Map of First Impressions in Models 6.1 and 6.2.

In the article I read and in my own experience, I realize that relationships are often jeopardized by the lack of clear communication. In "The Myth of Romantic Love," Scott Peck says that even when couples have fallen out of love, they tend to ignore that fact and hope that everything will work out all right. I had a similar experience with a girl I had been dating for about a year. I no longer had the feelings for her that I once did, and I wanted to change our relationship. However, I stifled my feelings and tried to go on. One day our relationship was destroyed in a terrible fight. It wasn't until two years later that we were able to sit down and talk it out. Since that experience, I have been trying to work on being honest and straightforward when I need to be.

—Michael "Cody" Brooks

COMMENT: Cody focuses on his own experience and on the way that the information in "The Myth of Romantic Love" relates to that experience. Notice that he begins his response with a clear topic sentence and then paraphrases one of the author's ideas before relating this idea to his own life.

MODEL 6.5: Essay Response to "Your Child's Self-Esteem"

Sometimes you may find that you have an extended response to an author's ideas and that your response is several paragraphs long. This is the case with the student response that follows "Your Child's Self-Esteem." Read the article, then the student response.

Your Child's Self-Esteem

by Lilian G. Katz

The idea that children should feel good about themselves is, remarkably, a relatively modern one. Only one or two generations ago, praise was withheld from children for fear that youngsters might become conceited or "swell-headed." These days, however, it often seems that we err to the other extreme, and many children are in danger of becoming too self-conscious and eager for praise.

It's not so difficult to understand how praising a child's efforts can positively affect his self-esteem, and parents may need little guidance in this regard. But parents may be less clear about how they affect a child's feelings about himself in other ways. With an eye toward helping parents with this dilemma, I've outlined some ideas below that you may want to consider as you think about developing a healthy sense of self-esteem in your child.

An individual's self-esteem is the result of evaluations by one's self and others. For young children, the greatest influences on self-esteem—high and low—are others' evaluations, especially those people closest to the child. The basis for self-esteem in childhood is the feeling of being loved and accepted, particularly by someone the child can look up to. This is one reason that parental support means so much to children and has such an extraordinary effect on the self-esteem.

Remember that it is not desirable to have excessive self-esteem. Indeed, an excessively high degree of self-esteem, confidence, or assurance might cause a person to be insensitive to others' reactions and feelings about him. Though it is difficult to know precisely where the level is, the optimum level of self-esteem seems to be that which allows for the normal fluctuations in feelings of confidence, pride, and competence. The actual complexities of life are sufficient that all children (and adults) encounter situations in which it is realistic to have little confidence, hurt pride, or insufficient competence. Children can be helped by adults to accept the fact that such difficult situations are inevitable. They are also temporary, and in the scheme of things, they are only a small portion of the range of experiences they'll have in life.

Self-esteem varies from one interpersonal situation to another. Children do not have to be accepted or loved by everyone they encounter. Parents can help a child cope with occasions of rejection or indifference by reassuring her that Mom's and Dad's own acceptance of the youngster has not been shaken.

Self-esteem is not acquired all at once early in life to last forever and be present in all situations. A child may feel confident and accepted at home but the opposite in the neighborhood or preschool. Adults can generally avoid those situations in which their self-esteem is likely to take a beating, but children are limited to situations adults provide for them. They have few skills or resources for avoiding situations in which their self-assurances will be threatened. Parents should be aware that in some instances inappropriate behavior on the part of their child may be a signal that the child perceives the particular circumstance as threatening to his self-confidence.

Self-esteem is measured against certain criteria, typically acquired within the family. The criteria against which we are evaluated vary among families, ethnic groups, and neighborhoods. They also vary for boys and girls—more so in some communities than in others. In some families or groups esteem is based on physical beauty, in others on intelligence, athleticism, or toughness. Your child will need help in meeting your standards on those criteria. Whatever criteria for being an acceptable person make sense in your family, support your child's effort to meet them, but reassure her that, no matter what, she is loved and always belongs to the family.

An Extended Response

Building Self-Esteem in Children With Learning Disabilities

Trying to build self-esteem in children with learning disabilities is one of the hardest responsibilities for a parent. The reason I know this is because two of my children have learning disabilities. It has been tough to build up their self-esteem only to have someone else knock it back down.

Children with learning disabilities are constantly being rejected by their peers because they're perceived as being different. My daughter had a friend in grade school, and because of peer pressure in middle school, her friend dumped her just so the others would accept her [the friend]. On my daughter's sixteenth birthday, nobody came to her party. Her self-esteem took a real beating that day, and I learned a valuable lesson. The two of us do something special together to celebrate her birthday from now on.

In "Your Child's Self-Esteem," Lilian G. Katz tells us that "Parents can help a child cope with occasions of rejection or indifference by reassuring her that Mom's and Dad's own acceptance of the youngster has not been shaken." I disagree that this is enough, especially with a learning-disabled child. Telling my children that I love them isn't what they want to hear; what matters to them is acceptance by their peers. I've tried to reinforce their good behavior and encourage them to see themselves as valuable human beings, but their peer acceptance means more than mine or their teachers'.

I have found that it helps to explain everything in detail to my children and avoid talking down to them. These techniques have helped to build their self-esteem. Although one of my responsibilities as a parent is to build self-esteem, I know I cannot provide the acceptance that they need from others, especially peers.

—Sandy Krepps (student)

COMMENT: Sandy has a good topic sentence in which she clearly disagrees with the author of "Your Child's Self-Esteem." Furthermore, Krepps uses the specific example of her daughter's birthday party to explain her position.

ACTIVITY 6.3

In Activity 6.1 you read "Men's Jobs, Women's Jobs" and wrote your initial impressions. Now write a response. Be sure to include a clear topic sentence.

ACTIVITY 6.4

In Chapter Four you read "The Importance of Childhood Memories" and saw a model that identifies the major details. Now brainstorm your reactions using either a list or a map. Then write a response.

Self-Check Review

1. What are two ways to record your first reactions to an article?
2. List three questions you can ask yourself to help organize your thinking.
3. What are two suggestions for writing the topic sentence of your response?
4. Why do you think it is valuable to respond to what you read?
5. How can you use the information in this chapter in school, at work, and in your personal life? ✦

Chapter Seven

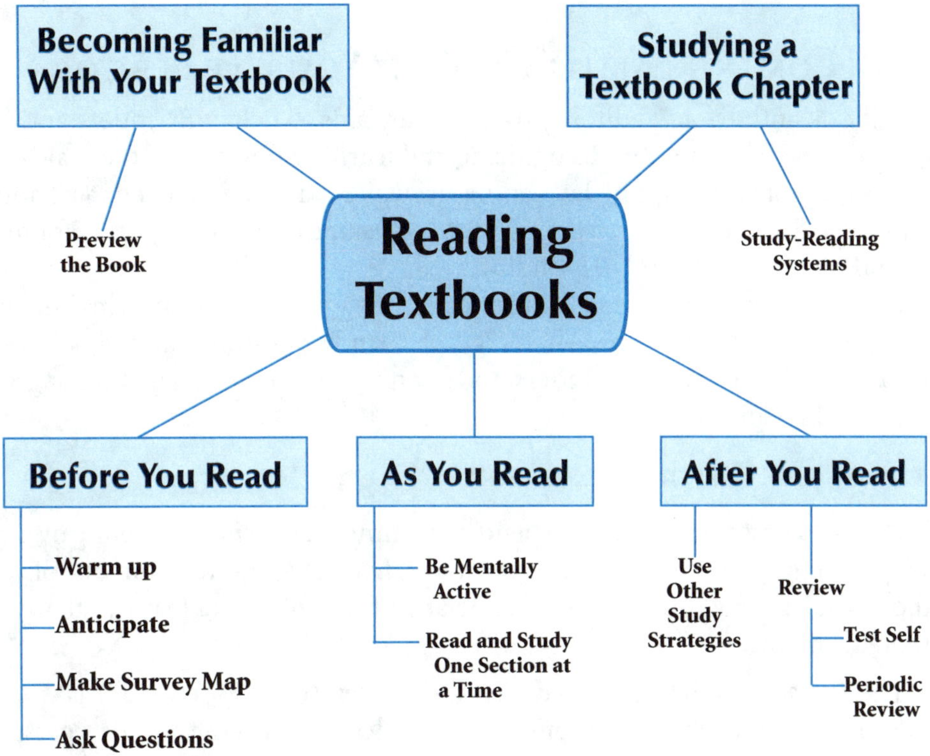

Textbooks present special reading challenges. Very often they include technical and specialized terms that are difficult to spell, pronounce, and remember. The chapters are often lengthy, and the relationships between chapters may be unclear. Despite these difficulties, you need to remember much of the material at test time, sometimes weeks after you have read it.

However, there are methods to help you understand and remember information in textbooks. Most students read a textbook just as they would a novel or a magazine article, but viewing a textbook as a source of information, much like a dictionary, is more effective. The basic rule to remember is this: Do not read your textbooks—"study" them.

The models and activities in this chapter will help you

- Identify the main ideas and major details in textbook chapters.
- Use a study-reading system to learn and remember textbook material.

Becoming Familiar With Your Textbook

Textbook authors and editors provide many aids to help you understand and remember new information. Recognizing and learning how to use these aids will make it easier for you to apply the reading strategies that you practiced in Chapters Two through Six: previewing to get an overview, asking questions, looking for main ideas and major details, and responding.

Most textbooks have special features such as headings (sometimes in different-sized type and color), pictures, charts, graphs, study questions, and glossaries to help you. Often you can better understand a concept by studying a picture or graph than by reading an explanation.

Preview the Entire Textbook

When you first get a textbook, spend some time *previewing* or looking over the entire book to get an overall idea of the subject. Look at a chapter from one of your textbooks; take a few minutes to examine any of the following features that your textbook contains.

- The *Preface* (sometimes titled "To the Student" or "Foreword") is usually found near the table of contents and provides you with the author's perspective on the subject. In this section, authors often explain their approach and the organization of the book. See the "To the Student" section in *Read and Respond* as an example of this feature.
- The *Contents,* found at the front of the book, lists the book's chapters. By viewing the chapter titles, you learn the various major topics of the book, and you can see how some of the topics are related. The table of contents can help you get a quick and valuable overview of the subject of your class.
- The *Index,* located at the end of the book, is an alphabetical listing of the topics, terms, and names mentioned in the book. Use this section to find the page on which a particular concept or person is discussed. It can help you find and mark main ideas and major details, which are strategies you practiced in Chapters Three and Four.
- A *Glossary* is a list of technical and specialized words in the book along with their definitions. In a textbook, glossary entries may be found at the end of a

chapter, at the end of the book, or in the margins of the text near the words they define.

- An *Appendix* presents additional information that can help you understand the book's subject matter. Found near the back of the book, appendices might include charts, graphs, special documents, or alternate views and approaches to the subject.
- *Questions, Problems,* or *Exercises,* typically found at the end of a chapter, provide practical application of the ideas in the chapter or things to look for as you read.

Studying a Textbook Chapter

Let's suppose you are assigned a chapter in your sociology text. If you are like most students, you will probably open the book to the first page of the chapter and start reading. But there is a better way. If you apply a textbook reading strategy, you will be able to read the chapter faster, and better yet, you will *understand* and *remember* the material better. Reading for understanding leads to better grades.

What Is a Study-Reading System?

A study-reading system is a step-by-step procedure for reading a textbook chapter. It can help you organize what you read for future study and review. Keep in mind that textbooks should not simply be read—they are to be studied.

Study-reading systems work. Research studies show that students who are taught to use a study-reading system understand and remember what they read much better than students who have not learned how to use a system.

The next few pages explain strategies for each of three stages involved in the process of studying college-level textbook chapters: *before you read, as you read,* and *after you read*. Following the explanation is a sample chapter from a sociology textbook. It provides models of how to mark a textbook and opportunities for you to practice the strategies.

Before You Read

Preview

Previewing a textbook chapter is a more extensive task than previewing an article. In the long run, however, it will save you a great deal of time and help you remember the information. It is critical that you recall what you already know about the topic and get a clear overview of the whole chapter **before** reading individual sections of the chapter.

Information and ideas you already have about a topic are called **prior knowledge** or **background knowledge.** This knowledge is as significant as what is written in the chapter, so it is very important to bring it to your conscious mind before you begin reading.

How do you do this?

Step One: Warm Up Your Thinking

- As you read the title and headings in bold type, jot down things you already know about each topic in the chapter. You might do this in the form of free-writing—jotting down whatever comes to your mind without worrying about grammar, punctuation, or paragraphing—or you might make a list of your thoughts. Another possibility is to put your thoughts in the form of a chart or a map.

  Any of these formats will help you recall what you already know about the topic. This preview *brainstorming* is very similar to the *first reaction* step you did before writing your response in Chapter Six. The obvious difference in this case is that you are writing your ideas and thoughts *before* you read the author's ideas.

- Continue this *warm-up* step by determining how many pages are in the chapter and how many major topics are covered. Major topics are usually indicated by the headings in the largest and darkest type. If the major headings and subheadings are not numbered, it is a good idea to use your own numbering system.

  One suggested method for numbering is demonstrated on pages 102–105. The numbers 1.0, 2.0, and so forth are used for the major headings. The subheadings are labeled 1.1, 1.2, and so forth. The first number corresponds with the major heading number and the second number indicates the subheading. Numbering the headings will help you keep track of all the parts of the chapter as well as help you organize your written notes in the *after reading* stage.

- Read the summary if there is one; the summary usually contains the author's most important points. Also pay attention to any illustrations, graphs, charts, or other special features in the chapter. If you know very little about the topic, continue with the rest of the steps in the preview, then come back to this step and try free-writing again.

ACTIVITY 7.1

Working in groups, preview the sample chapter from a sociology textbook entitled "Mating and Marrying," which starts on page 101.

1. Which of the following special features does the chapter have? Give a page number for each feature you locate.

   Boldface theadings

   Preview questions

   Main topics of the chapter

   Main ideas of the chapter

   Pictures

   Graphs

   Charts

   Vocabulary words

   Summary

   Other (write the type of feature and the page number)
2. Read the information in Box 8.1 on page 119, and Box 8.2 on page 120. This information is separated from the rest of the chapter by the boxes around it and the shaded background. It is a good idea to read supplemental information such as that contained in these boxes when you preview a chapter. Many times this information is of special interest or raises questions for you. In Box 8.1, for instance, are you familiar with the idea of the male in a heterogeneous couple spending more time "in the kitchen" and helping with childcare?
3. Look at the glossary on pages 123 and 124. When might you refer to this list of words and definitions?
4. Notice the small icon in the shape of a computer at the end of many sections. See pages 122 and 123. How could you use these Internet website references?

Step Two: Anticipate the Chapter Contents

As you think about the title and headings, make a brief list of what you think the author will discuss.

ACTIVITY 7.2

Complete your preview of "Mating and Marrying" by answering the following questions about the chapter.

1. Reread the chapter title, headings, and introduction on pages 101 and 102. What is the general topic of this chapter? What is the specific topic of the chapter?
2. What do you already know about this topic? Write any information in the form of a list, a map, or a freewrite.
3. How many pages are there in the chapter? How many headings? Number the headings and subheadings for the rest of the chapter (see pages 102–105 as a model).
4. Read the last full paragraph on page 122, labeled "Conclusion." Often concluding paragraphs are called a summary. Did you identify it as a summary in Activity 7.1? Why is it important to look for a summary and read it as a part of your preview?
5. Read the captions under the pictures and charts.
6. If you know very little about this topic, look over the chapter quickly two or three times. Then write any additional information that you now have in response to question 2.

Step Three: Make a Survey Map

In addition to identifying the major topics in the chapter, it is important to understand the relationships between those topics.

ACTIVITY 7.3

Compare the survey map for this chapter, on page 85, with the maps at the beginning of Chapters One through Six. In groups, list the similarities and differences between the Chapter Seven map and those for Chapters One through Six.

What Is a Survey Map?

A survey map is a picture that connects the chapter headings and subheadings by means of lines and shapes to show the relationships between them. Creating a survey map builds on Step One of previewing. Write the headings and subheadings that you read on a clean piece of paper, where there is plenty of space for you to show their relationships. As you probably discovered in Activity 7.3, a map may take any one of a variety of forms. We have used two forms for the survey maps at the beginning of chapters in this book. Chapters One through Six have maps with the chapter title at the top in a box and the major headings listed under it (see Model 7.1).

MODEL 7.1

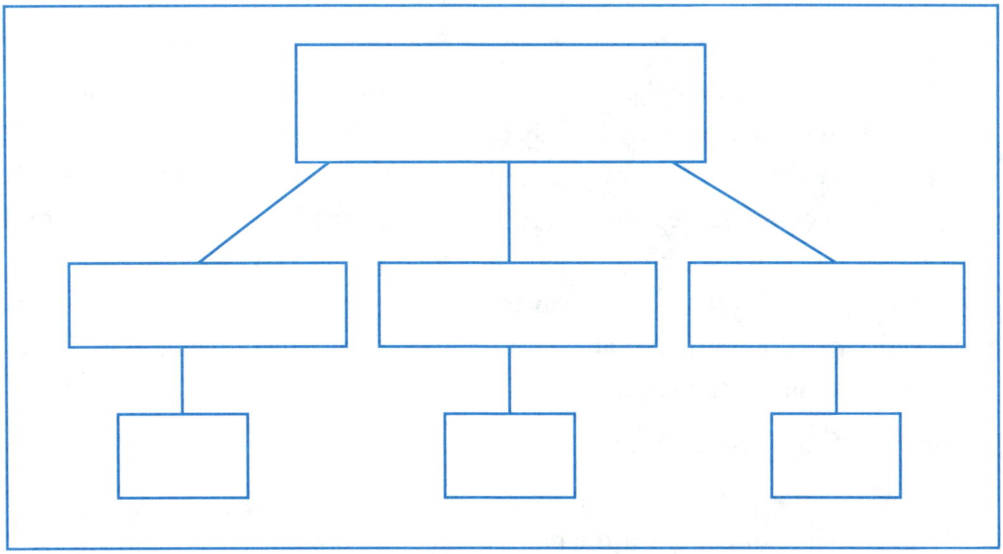

The map on the first page of Chapter Seven begins with the chapter title written in a circle or box in the center. The headings and subheadings are branched around it (see Model 7.2).

MODEL 7.2

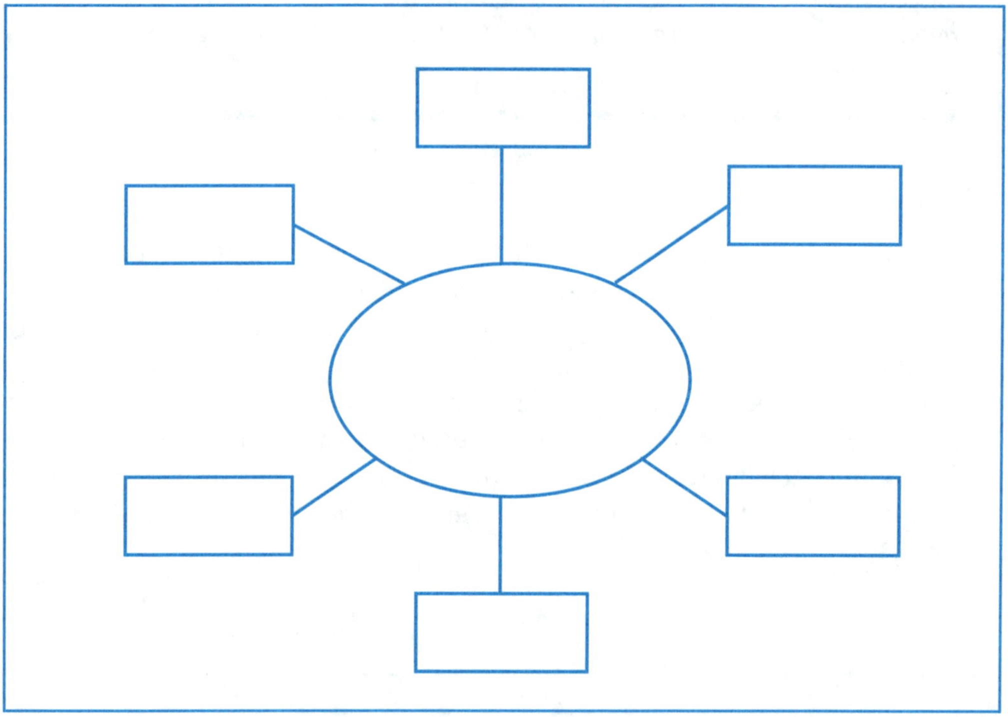

COMMENT: When you make a survey map, be sure that all the words run in the same direction so that they will be easy to read and follow. Many students find it helpful to use different colors of pencil or ink to distinguish major headings and subheadings. You might need to try a couple of different drawings before you find a layout that works well. Like any technique, this one will be easier after you practice it a few times. There is no one way to make a survey map; use your own ideas and creativity to draw a map that is meaningful to you. The important thing is to clearly show all of the topics in the chapter and how they relate to each other.

How to Make a Survey Map

- Write the title of the chapter at the top or in the center of a piece of paper. Use a whole piece of paper for the map so that you have plenty of room.

- Next, write down the chapter headings and indicate their relationship to the chapter title. Usually, this relationship is shown by putting the headings in boxes or circles that are somewhat smaller than the one for the chapter title and then connecting them to the title with lines.
- Draw lines from the circles and boxes containing the headings to each of the subheadings.

ACTIVITY 7.4

Begin a survey map for the sociology chapter on pages 102 to 125 by putting the chapter title at the top or in the center of the page. Next, look at the chapter headings; the sample chapter has four:

Family Systems Across Space and Time
Mate Selection in Modern Society
The Modern American Family
Family and Household Diversity in Contemporary America

Write these headings in boxes or circles and add them to your map, connecting them with lines to the chapter title.

This may seem like a lot to do before reading, but remember that the more you do before you begin, the easier and better your reading will be. You will also remember the information better and have a tool to use later for review.

Step Four: Ask Questions

Textbook reading involves getting answers to questions. The preview step will generate a lot of questions; you can create additional questions by **turning headings into questions.**

Headings in a chapter are answers to specific questions. Use the headings to figure out a question for each section. Often, the chapter will also have subheadings that divide the material under a heading into sections. If subheadings are provided, ask questions for them as well. Always try to determine how the sections and subsections relate to each other.

MODEL 7.3: Creating Questions for Chapter Headings

The first heading of the sociology chapter is "Family Systems Across Space and Time." Appropriate questions for this section might be, What is a family system? and How have family systems changed over time?

Another way to figure out a question for a heading is to preview the section by reading the first sentence of every paragraph. These beginning sentences usually provide a **signal-word** to announce the main topic of the paragraph. For example, read the first sentence of the fourth paragraph on page 102. The word "another" signals a transition to an additional principle of social life: the rule of reciprocity. Similarly, the first sentence of the first paragraph on page 103 contains a signal-word phrase, "A third cultural foundation of marriage." This signal-word phrase indicates that third principle of social life: the principle of legitimacy. Appropriate questions for this section might be, What are social or cultural principles of family systems? and How are they defined?

ACTIVITY 7.5

Write two questions for each of the remaining major headings in this chapter (see pages 107 and 113).

As You Read

Read Actively

The suggestions in Steps One and Two of the "Before You Read" section will help you read actively; by previewing, you **focus** your mind; by asking questions and looking for answers to those questions, you **maintain your focus.**

As you read, the important thing is to make sense of the material, so you will probably need to read a textbook more *slowly* than you read other kinds of books.

Tackle One Major Section at a Time

You have already discovered how the chapter is organized by designing a survey map. Keep your survey map in front of you to help keep track of the "big picture" of the chapter as you focus on one major section at a time.

Here are some additional suggestions to help you read **actively:**

1. **Look for the answers to the questions you asked in your preview.** When you think you have found an answer, write it down on a piece of notebook paper or in the margin of your textbook.
2. **Look for other questions to be answered.** Write questions about words or concepts you don't know, or don't understand. Try to find the answers to those questions.
3. **Look for main ideas** of paragraphs and sections under each heading and subheading.
4. **Think about important points or sections that do not make sense.** You may need to look up words in the glossary or a dictionary, refer to your lecture notes, or talk to a study partner to help clarify the meaning of a paragraph or section.
5. **Mark the text as you read** with a pencil or an ink pen rather than a highlighter pen; marking with a highlighter is passive, and you are working to become an **active** reader. An active reader may do the following:
   a. Divide sections into subsections. When there are no boldface headings in a chapter, you will need to divide the text into sections and subsections, identifying the topic of each section in the margin. Basically, you will be doing the same thing you did with longer articles in Chapter Four.
   b. Divide the sections by drawing lines.
   c. Label the sections. Sometimes the heading will work; other times you will need to write a new heading for a section, divide it into smaller sections, or write a heading for each subsection.
   d. Put a check mark or an X in the margin beside any new or special words you want to learn and remember.
   e. Underline the main ideas of the paragraphs or sections. Be careful not to underline too much (no more than 10 to 20 percent of a page) in order to stay focused on main ideas.

MODEL 7.4: Markings and Notes in a Sample Textbook Chapter

Turn to pages 102–105 of the sample sociology chapter. Notice that key points are in boldface type and that Section 1.0 has two subheadings. Pay attention to notes written in the margins.

ACTIVITY 7.6

Read Section 2.0, "Mate Selection in Modern Society," on pages 105–107. Label the subsections and write the topic of each subsection in the margin. Divide the subsection entitled "The Marriage Market" into sections and label each part in the margin. Underline the main idea of any paragraphs or subsections and make notes in the margin that you think might be helpful for studying the chapter. Compare your sections and marginal notes with a classmate's or discuss them with your instructor.

After You Read

Study the Information in the Chapter You Have Just Read

Earlier in this chapter, you learned that a basic rule of textbook reading is to *study* textbooks, not just *read* them. Previewing and asking questions are a part of studying. Equally important is what you do after you finish reading each section.

There are many ways to study the information. The strategy demonstrated here is an extension of the strategy you practiced in Chapter Four—making a **summary outline** of what you read.

MODEL 7.5: Sample Summary Outline of a Textbook Chapter

Topic: Family systems across space and time, *OR*, The family as a socially constructed institution

1.0 Main Idea: Socially acceptable norms in a family have a great deal to do with sexual attraction and set cultural foundations.

Major Details:

1.1 Important principles of social life that affect family systems

Incest taboos vary from culture to culture but are an important way of controlling family systems

Rules of reciprocity create stronger ties between kinship groups

Social fatherhood: father takes responsibility for children and wife even if he is not the biological father

1.2 Traditional vs. modern societies' perspectives

Traditional societies: mate selection and other family issues are based on what is best for the kinship group, not the nuclear family

Historical view of the family: kinship group = extended family

Modern societies: nuclear family is separate and self-sufficient from other nuclear units

Emotional bonds are the strength *and* the weakness of nuclear family system

In America, most people have lived in a nuclear family system

COMMENT: Sometimes, if the material you are reading seems very difficult, you will need to do a summary outline on each section of the chapter. Other times, the notes you write in the margin of your text will be sufficient to help you understand and remember the information.

ACTIVITY 7.7

Write a main idea statement in your own words for sections 3.0 and 4.0 of the sample sociology textbook chapter. In Activity 7.6, you identified the topic of each section. Now write the main point the authors are making about the topic of each section. Then, write the major details in each section that explain or support the authors' main point.

Use Other Study Strategies

The following list provides suggestions and models of textbook reading strategies. Your instructor may have other suggestions. The important thing is to condense textbook material and put it into your own words without changing the original meaning.

1. **Make a more detailed map** of the entire chapter. After completing a survey map, make a map of each major section of the chapter. Visual learners often prefer this method.
2. **Turn headings into questions,** and write the answers to these questions. This method is sometimes referred to as SQ3R, SQ4R, or PQRST.
3. **Make flashcards** of key terms and special vocabulary that are unfamiliar to you (see Chapter Two).
4. **Answer questions** from a study guide. Some instructors make up study guides to help you identify the most important information in the chapter; other times, a study guide is available when you buy your textbook.
5. **Create a chart** of the information. A chart is another form of a map with the added feature of categorizing and comparing two or more items. Some information is easier to study in a chart, and you can easily quiz yourself from a chart. Charts, like maps, have various formats. The chart in Model 7.6 was created by a student taking a logic class, and the chart in Model 7.7 was made by a student in a biology class.

MODEL 7.6: Logic Class—Fallacies Everyone Should Know

No.	Name	Explanation	Example
1	*Bifurcation/ False Dichotomy*	Giving an either/or scenario without giving any choice for in-between possibilities; disposition to mistake contrary predicates for complementary ones.	Either you're for national security or you're for terrorism.
2	*Slippery Slope*	Presuming a certain chain of events will inevitably ensue from a particular cause.	Outlawing pornography is a violation of our freedom of expression and soon the government will take away all of our constitutional rights.
3	*Ad Hominem Abusive*	Attacking the arguer, not the argument; to vilify, deride, or mock a person without addressing the merits or demerits of his or her argument.	Feminists are too lazy to engage in rigorous logic, and therefore their judgment cannot be trusted on this matter.
4	*Straw Man/ Distortion*	Instead of rebutting a position, reinterpreting it to make it more vulnerable to attack; interpreting a position in a way that makes yours more favorable.	A: I think we should lower our defense budgets. B: A wants to weaken our national defense system.
5	*Appeal to Pity*	Trying to elude sympathy from the opponent; use of emotionally charged language; appealing to emotion.	I come from a poor family in a small town and have had to work my way up; therefore, I deserve this promotion.

Model 7.7: Biology Study Chart

	Dicot Root	Monocot Root	Dermal Tissue	Vascular Tissue	Stem Tissue	Leaf Structure
Contains Epidermal Cells	X	X	X		X	X
Contains Apical Meristem	X	X			X	
Includes a Vascular Ring	X					X
Made of Palisade and Spongy Mesophyll	X					
Contains Parenchyma Cells	X	X	X	X	X	X
Contains Xylem and Phloem				X	X	X
Contains Stomota						X
Contains Plasmodesmota	X	X	X	X	X	X

Review

To review, look over what you have read. Read aloud to yourself or a partner everything you've written in the margins. Cover up your written answers to questions and major details in your summary outline, and test yourself to see if you can recall them.

It is also a good idea to refer to your **survey map** at this point. See how much you can recall about each major heading without looking at your notes. Turn to page 85 for the survey map for this chapter. Test yourself on the ideas in this chapter by looking only at the information in the boxes. Next, cover up the information beneath each box, and recall as much of the information as you can about each phase of textbook reading.

The **first** review should take place when you finish the entire chapter. This will help you remember the material very well for approximately one day. You need to review a **second** time within one day. Your review can be as short as five to ten minutes. This review will probably help you remember the information for a week. A **third** review should take place within a week (again, five to ten minutes will probably be enough time). Finally, review again after one month. This will help you retain the information permanently in your long-term memory.

Periodic reviews will help you remember what you learn. Before a test, you will just need to review, not relearn, the material.

ACTIVITY 7.8

Self-Check Review

Look at the survey map that you made for the sample sociology textbook chapter (Activity 7.4). Test yourself on this information by looking at the major headings and recalling as much information as you can about "mating" and "marrying." On a blank piece of paper write "mating," then write everything you can remember about that topic. Do the same thing with the word "marrying."

1. What is the difference between textbook reading and other reading?
2. What are the three stages in the textbook reading process?
3. What do you do in the "Before You Read" stage of the textbook reading process?
4. What do you do in the "Reading" stage?
5. What are some strategies you could use to take notes in the "After Reading" stage?
6. How can you use the information in this chapter in school, at work, and in your personal life? ✦

Sample Chapter from a Sociology Textbook

Mating and Marrying: Contemporary Families

❖ ❖ ❖ ❖

Intro—importance of family system and idea of family as socially constructed system.

Every society must deal with two major survival issues: controlling sexual impulses and pairing off members for orderly reproduction. The solution to both problems is the set of rules and roles that govern mate selection and marriage—the **family system**. Groups which devised norms that most people could follow survived, while groups that failed to regulate sexuality or ensure marital stability disappeared. The result is a world with hundreds of different family systems, each of which claims to be the one normal, natural, and sacred way of mating and marrying. In other words, family life is neither divinely ordained nor biologically programmed. The family is a socially constructed institution, as much a product of culture and history as political or economic systems (Farrell 1999; Coltrane 1998). This chapter examines such central aspects of marriage and family as:

- Cross-cultural and historical variations.
- Mate selection in modern societies.
- Modern marriage.
- Family diversity in America.
- The new family life cycle.

Family Systems Across Space and Time

Unique Human Family

The human family differs from the ties that link our primate cousins because of the unique qualities of culture such as language and norms, and the human qualities of foresight and self-control. The first and most powerful norms were those that directed sexual attraction into socially helpful patterns, namely the **incest taboos** that forbid sexual relations among blood relatives or kin. Although the taboo is found in all existing societies, there is great variation as to which relatives are covered. Sometimes the taboo involves only parents and children and brothers and sisters; in other societies individuals even remotely related are forbidden to mate. In a few instances, members of a ruling elite were expected to marry a close relative in order to keep the family property intact.

Cultural Foundation
a. Incest Taboos
b. Rule of Reciprocity
c. Legitimacy Principle

By forbidding sexuality within the kinship group, three important social goals are accomplished: (1) jealousy among people who live together is reduced, (2) doubt about how members are related to one another is eliminated, and (3) young people are forced to look elsewhere for marriage partners. A fourth benefit was accidental, namely, a lowered incidence of mental and physical disorders caused by inbreeding. The most important immediate consequence of incest taboos, in the earliest human societies and right up to modern times, was to forge alliances between kinship groups. There is a sense in which the 1960s bumper sticker, "Make Love, Not War," represents one of the earliest social insights: It is better to establish ties of mutual obligation than to create enemies.

The exchange of sons and daughters as marriage partners illustrates another important principle of social life: the **rule of reciprocity**, whereby to receive a gift is to be obligated to return something of equal value. If you give your daughter to my son in marriage, we are forever mutually obligated. The giving of presents before and during a marriage, today as well as in the past,

❖ ❖ ❖ ❖

serves to link the families and the couple to one another and to the larger community.

A third cultural foundation of marriage is based on the **principle of legitimacy**, or **social fatherhood**, whereby one man, the husband, is responsible for his wife's children, whether or not he is their biological father. Having a social father ensures that the child will be looked after materially. This is important in societies where a father's status determines the social location of his children. Where there is little to inherit, it matters little whose child you are, which is why illegitimacy rates are higher among the poor than the wealthy—not because the poor have looser morals but because legitimacy confers few advantages. For people with property, it makes a big difference who inherits it.

1.1 Kinship in Cross-Cultural Perspective

Kinship, or relationships based on descent and marriage, was the central organizing principle of most societies before the rise of the nation-state. In the days before centralized governments could guarantee social order, people depended on their kin for protection, and when most people made a living on the land, the kinship group was an economic unit. It was crucially important for family honor and wealth that your child marry someone whose family connections could benefit the kinship group. The last thing you want as a family elder is to have your careful plans upset by a child who falls in love with an inappropriate partner. For these reasons, in many societies even today, daughters are kept under tight supervision, and the choice of a marriage partner for both sons and daughters is made by the parents. You may not have to go too far back in your own family history to find an example of an arranged marriage. 💻 1

Evolution of Kinship-based family to Nation-state.

Wide variety of differences dependent on culture and time period.

As you can see in Table 8.1, mate selection is only one dimension on which traditional and modern societies differ. The variations on these essential elements, along with patterns of child rearing, divorce, and widowhood, mean that no two family systems are exactly alike. The only common thread in preindustrial societies is the supreme importance of the kinship group rather than the individual members. In modern societies, where your eventual position in the social world is not totally dependent on that of your parents, you have more room to negotiate your own choice of mate. If you are not waiting for your father to die in order to inherit the farm, you do not have to be quite as obedient.

1.2 The Family in Historical Context

The kinship group that so dominates its members is often described as an **extended family**, a unit composed of related households sharing economic tasks and providing support in illness and old age.

In contrast, the modern family is one in which the emphasis shifts to individuals, to the well-being of the couple and that of their children in the **nuclear family**. Industrialization erodes the power of family elders; young adults leave the village for the city and make their own way in the world. There are police forces to protect you, schools to educate you, and places of worship that you share with nonrelatives. The ties that bind the generations are no longer based on duty but on affection, which must be earned rather

Two types of families: Extended and Nuclear (Nuclear is more modern).

Table 8.1 Kinship in Cross-Cultural Perspective

	Traditional Societies	Modern Societies
Number of spouses at one time	One (**monogamy**) or plural (**polygamy**) **Polygyny**—two or more wives **Polyandry**—two or more husbands	One (**monogamy**)
Choice of spouse	Choices made by parents to enhance family power	Relatively free choice
Line of descent (inheritance)	From males (**patrilineal**) From females (**matrilineal**)	Both equally (**bilateral kinship**)
Couple's home	With groom's family (**patrilocal**) With bride's family (**matrilocal**)	Place of one's own (**neolocal**)
Power relationships	Various degrees of male dominance (**patriarchy**)	Greater equality (**egalitarian**)
Functions of family	All-embracing, to protect the kinship group as a whole	Specialized to provide a stable environment for child rearing and emotional support
Structure	Extended	Nuclear
Focus of obligation	Blood relationships	Marriage tie and children

than commanded. The functions of family are reduced to those related to physical and emotional well-being within the privacy of the nuclear household (Waite 2000).

Nuclear family's strength is also its weakness.

It is this separateness and self-sufficiency that distinguishes the modern family from nuclear units of the past. The central relationship is the marriage rather than the bloodline. If, for example, two messengers arrived simultaneously at the door of today's young wife, one with word that her father was gravely ill at hospital X and the other with news that her husband had had an accident and was at hospital Y, where would she go first? Most likely to the side of her spouse; in contrast, someone from a traditional society, particularly a son, would probably go to his father's bedside.

Unfortunately, the same emotional bonds that are the strength of the nuclear family system are also a source of weakness. Remember Georg Simmel's description of the essential fragility of the dyad (chapter 1)? When the affection that holds it together is lost, what is left? The modern family is an extremely vulnerable institution, but not many young people today would prefer the extended family alternatives.

The vision of generations of happy kin living together—the "family of Western nostalgia" (Coontz 1992)—is more wishful thinking than historical reality. In America, and in much of Western Europe from the eighteenth century on, most people lived in nuclear units, perhaps joined temporarily by a widowed grandparent. There is no reason to believe that past generations of parents and children desired to live together any more than they do today. As told in the Greek plays of 2,500 years ago and throughout the Bible, family relations have always been marked by fear, jealousy, sibling hostility, and murders of parents by children and children by parents.

20

Mate Selection in Modern Society

When the goal of marriage is personal fulfillment and emotional well-being, then you must be free to select your mate on the basis of personal attraction. Thus, the ideal of *romantic love* emerged as the only legitimate rationale for mate selection in modern societies. Think how difficult it would be to justify your choice of marriage partner with any reason other than "I love him/her," even if you were doing it for the money or social status. True, there are tales of romantic love from olden times, but usually tragic ones: Romeo and Juliet do not ride off into the sunset, nor did Tristan and Isolde live happily ever after. Perhaps the poor could marry for love, but not the powerful and wealthy.

Marrying for love has its hazards. Few of us are perfect judges of character. The excitement of the moment can blind us to destructive faults. A lifetime of bliss is probably more than should be expected of any relationship. Indeed, it is precisely the difficulty of achieving personal fulfillment through marriage that accounts for the high divorce rates in modern societies. If you married only out of duty to kin, your expectation level might be low enough to enable you to endure situations that would be unacceptable to you today. But when you marry for love, just "getting by" is not enough.

The Pool of Eligibles

Even though you are essentially out there on your own in search of a partner, your parents have not been powerless. They have already influenced your choice in a number of ways: by where they lived, what church they joined, and which extracurricular activities they encouraged. Your parents are also inside your head; think of the last person to whom you were strongly attracted before a little voice told you that this was not someone you could bring home to dinner. To the extent that your parents serve as role models, you will look for similar qualities in a prospective mate—someone of the same race, religion, ethnicity, and social class. People who are like you in terms of background characteristics will have shared similar socialization experiences, which means that you will

Peter J. Stein

An increasing number of American marriages are heterogamous with respect to ethnicity and religion. Why is this happening?

agree on a lot of issues. And surely you have noticed that people who agree with you are smarter and nicer than those who disagree.

For all these reasons, although you are theoretically free to marry anyone who catches your fancy, your selection is generally limited to those you meet and can confidently introduce to relatives and friends. These considerations automatically reduce your "pool of eligibles" to those who are not all that different from yourself. The tendency to pick a partner who shares your ascribed characteristics—race, religion, ethnicity, and social class—is called **homogamy** (from "homo"= "same" and "gamy"= "marriage").

At the same time, young people today are able to travel a lot farther from home, at an earlier age, and more frequently than in the past, so the chances of meeting someone different from yourself have increased. As a consequence, in terms of ethnicity and religion especially, an increasing number of marriages are **heterogamous** ("hetero"= "different"). The risks in heterogamy are value conflicts and misunderstandings arising from different socialization experiences. The plus side is that the partners are exposed to other ways of thinking and behaving, which should expand their range of tolerance and adaptability.

Although the importance of religion and ethnicity have diminished, race remains a powerful factor. For example, black/white marriages comprised only three of every 1,000 U.S. marriages in 1980 and only six in 1998—a 100 percent increase but still not very many people. In any event, as shown in Table 8.2, most interracial marriages involve "others," primarily Asian-Americans. 2

Table 8.2 Married Couples of Same or Mixed Races, 1980 and 1998

(Number per 1,000 marriages)

	1980	1998
White/white	903.4	869
Black/black	67.5	70
Black/white	3	6
White/other	9	17
Black/other	1	1
All other couples	16.1	37

Source: *Statistical Abstract of the United States, 1999,* p. 58.

The Marriage Market

When marriages are not arranged, women and men must make the best bargain they can. The word "bargain" is used intentionally because mate selection has many characteristics of the marketplace, where sellers advertise their best qualities and buyers look for the best value. Your market value is based on what others are willing to pay for, and despite all the changes of recent decades, that is still youth and beauty in women and earning ability in men, as illustrated in the market for donor eggs and sperm described in chapter 4, or the "Personals" column in your local newspaper. This means that a woman's market value declines over time, while a man's typically increases. The process was perfectly illustrated by the smash-hit TV program *Who*

Wants to Marry a Multi-Millionaire?, in which 50 young women in bathing suits competed for a marriage proposal from a middle-aged millionaire. The man and the woman he chose met and married in front of the cameras in prime time. Unfortunately for the producers, the groom had been less than honest about his background, and the couple split as soon as they returned from the honeymoon.

Social class is another major determinant of market value. Although most people will marry within their class level, a man can "marry down" since it is his achieved status that locates the couple in the class hierarchy. A woman, however, is under great pressure to marry at the same level as her father or to try to move up; otherwise, she will lose social status. Those of you with a sibling of the opposite sex know this very well. When a daughter announces that she has just met the nicest guy, her mother probably asks, "Where does he live, dear?" because it really matters and the mother has a social-class map of the community engraved in her head. The son who has just met the nicest gal is usually asked, with a wink, "What does she look like?"

The market is especially difficult for a woman with high educational and occupational statuses; there are not many unmarried men at her class level and the men can always marry down. By the same token, men at the lowest ranks of the educational and occupational hierarchies will have difficulty finding a woman willing to marry them. This is why high-ranked women and low-status men are overrepresented among the never-married.

The mate market is also sensitive to numbers. Where there is a shortage of one sex or the other, people will marry across lines of age and even race. For example, a shortage of young white women in the Western states in the nineteenth century led to many marriages between young men and older women or between white men and Native American women. Today, in African-American communities where women outnumber men yet have few opportunities to marry across racial lines, many will remain single. In other words, that black women are twice as likely as white women to be unmarried is primarily related to a shortage of marriageable men (Franklin 1997).

Nevertheless, over 90 percent of American men and women somehow manage to find a mate—for a longer or shorter period. Marriage certainly has not gone out of style.

The Modern American Family

The modern family differs in both structure (the private nuclear household) and function (emotional well-being) from the family of traditional societies. Indeed, the structure is essential to the function. In addition, contemporary American families also differ from the nuclear models of the 1950s and 1960s along such crucial dimensions as age at first marriage, power relationships, and risk factors for divorce and remarriage. 3

Age at First Marriage

The most dramatic change is the increasing age of first marriage for both women and men over the past half-century, as seen in Figure 8.1.

Figure 8.1 Median Age at First Marriage, United States, 1890-2000, by Sex

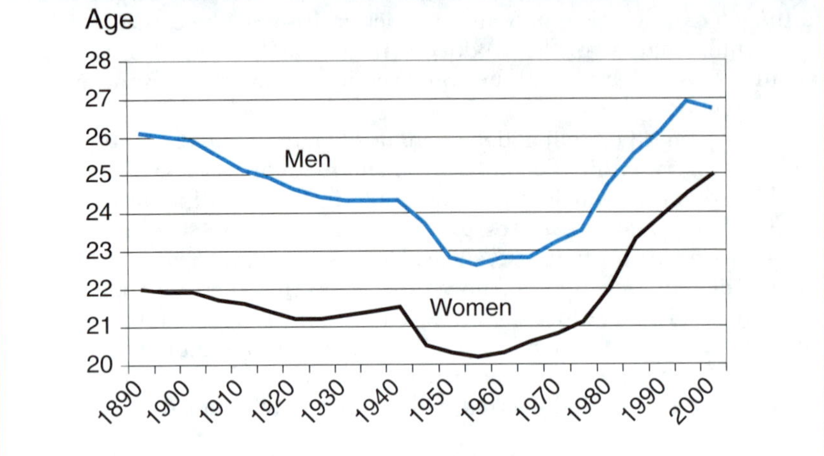

Source: U.S. Bureau of the Census. Internet release, January 1999.

Until World War II, marriage was typically delayed until the husband-to-be could support a family. By the late 1940s, however, young men could be supported by parents or the GI Bill for veterans while completing their education. Even college educated women were marrying before or right after graduation. Others went directly from high school to the altar. In the 1950s, close to half of all American women were married by age 20!

The nation was drowning in domesticity. Low-cost veterans' mortgages led to the development of suburban housing tracts (chapter 15); the birthrate shot up; and functional theorist Talcott Parsons (see chapter 1) could marvel at the harmonious division of labor in the modern nuclear family. Television shows featured mothers in aprons, fathers of infinite wisdom, and adoring children, not to mention the dog and cat, and the house with a picket fence and one-car garage.

In the 1960s, some of the glow had worn off. Divorce rates were creeping upward; the college-age children were experimenting with pot and alternative life-styles; and mother was marching for women's rights. By 1980, the median age at first marriage had risen two years, up to where it had been in 1890. In 1998, by age 25, only half of American women were married, while the median age at first marriage for men reached a historical high of 26.7 (Bureau of the Census, 1999).

The basic factor in this dramatic shift was the feminist movement and the new world of possibilities opened to women. Families were increasingly willing to pay for a daughter's college education; occupational choices opened up; independence was within reach; and marriage could be delayed, especially since the availability of effective contraceptives took much of the risk out of sexual relationships. As a result, young women were entering college, staying to graduate, taking jobs, seeing the world, and living on their own for several years before marriage (Kramer 2001).

Egalitarianism

Another way in which the contemporary family differs from that of a generation ago is in the reduction of power differences between husband and wife and between parents and children. To some extent, this trend toward **egalitarianism** is also a product of modern feminism, but a more basic factor is that the goal of mutual respect is incompatible with relationships of superiority and inferiority—superiors tend to get arrogant, and inferiors tend to lose self-respect. It is doubtful that slaves love their masters as much as the masters like to believe. What this means is that marriage partners and children and parents must earn rather than demand respect and affection.

Modern Marriage: Rewards and Risks

In general, married people are happier and healthier than the nonmarried (Waite and Gallagher 2000). Although people tend to think of men as less in need of marriage than women, husbands derive somewhat greater benefits than do wives in terms of physical and mental health, sexual satisfaction, and occupational success. Compared with their nonmarried peers, married men are very much better off (Nock 1998). Married men live longer than the unmarried and are far less likely to commit suicide, be homicide victims, die in accidents, or end up in mental health institutions. For women, the difference in death rates and health status between married and unmarried is much smaller than for men. The major problems for nonmarried women are financial. These trends are magnified by race, with black men particularly vulnerable to early death and black women overrepresented among the poor.

Yet for all the benefits of marriage, the closeness of the nuclear family can make it an emotional hothouse. People who are intensely dependent on one another for all their interpersonal needs are also very vulnerable.

Violence

As there are no accurate data from before the 1970s, it is impossible to say whether family life has become more or less violent. It can be argued that the lack of family privacy in the past made it easier for relatives and others in the community to intervene in cases of physical assault. But it is just as likely that the great power imbalances between husband and wife and parents and children encouraged abuses. What can be said for certain is that a lot of what was once acceptable disciplining in families is no longer tolerated.

This change in the public temper is due to the work of advocates for women and for children's' rights over the past three decades (Straus 2000). Although men are often targets of abuse from wives or girlfriends, the more common and most serious incidents involve women as victims (Kurz 2001). Both women and children are prime targets because outbursts of violence in the home are typically related to threats to authority. Men who feel powerless (especially at the hands of a woman) and parents who think they are being mocked can lose their cool very quickly. Despite claims that family violence cuts across class lines, it is strongly associated with low educational and occupational status, early marriage, and unplanned pregnancy (Gelles 1997). The incidence of physical abuse of women and children is also relatively high among members of groups that demand absolute obedience, such as the military and extremely religious communities (Schmidt 1994).

Does violence in the home matter? Very much, for children. Being the target of an abusive parent has a number of negative consequences—from a higher probability of becoming a juvenile delinquent to being violent with one's own wife and children (Swinford et al. 2000). It is safe to say that nothing good comes from hitting children, even with the best of intentions. The boys tend to become brutalized and the girls to be depressed (see chapter 3).

The most common and serious incidence of violence involves women as victims. Women are increasingly speaking and acting out against such violence.

The low esteem of abused daughters can make them unwitting targets for later violence. However, a girl need not have grown up in a violent home to feel that, as a woman, she is responsible for the emotional well-being of her husband or boyfriend, so that when anything goes wrong, she blames herself for whatever is driving him to violence. For many women, just having a man in her life is an affirmation of femininity. Here are some of the reasons that women typically give for staying with someone who hits them: "He's O.K. when he doesn't drink," "I really should stop nagging," "He's awfully sorry afterward," and "What are my choices?" They cannot go home to parents who will say "We told you so." There are not many shelters, and those are only for temporary use. Taking children out of school is difficult. Thus, many will stay and hope things will change, although they rarely do (Kurz 2001).

Increasingly, however, women are taking steps to leave abusive relationships, to become self-sufficient, and to use the police and courts to protect themselves. In addition, law enforcement agencies are being trained to be more sensitive to the dynamics of family violence and to be more helpful to the victims, female or male, young or old. 4

Divorce

Much that has been written about the American divorce rate is not accurate. The rate at which marriages break up has *not* risen for at least three decades. As you can see in Figure 8.2, there was a sharp upturn in divorces in the late 1940s, most likely due to hasty wartime marriages or marriages that could not survive a long separation. Then came two decades of low divorce rates, with another up-tick in the late 1970s before leveling off and even dropping in the late 1990s.

Figure 8.2 Marriage and Divorce Rates, U.S. 1930–1998 (Rate per 1000 population)

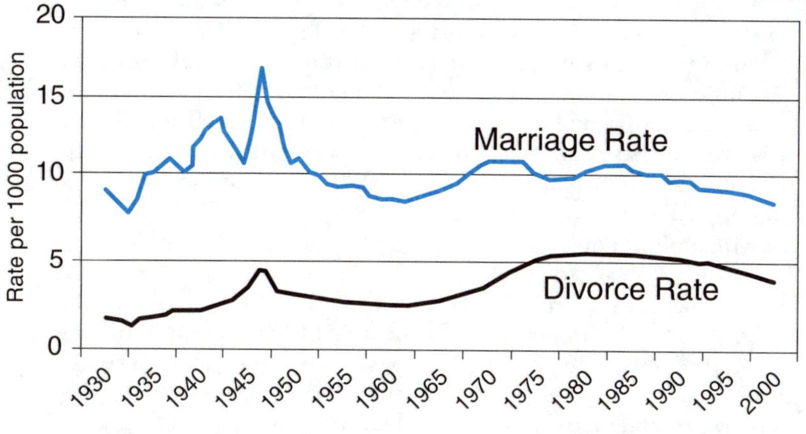

Source: *Monthly Vital Statistics Report*, Vol. 43(1), 1994; Vol. 48(5), 2000.

Predictors. The answer to questions of why divorce rates have remained stable or even declined since 1970 is contained in Figure 8.1: *Median age at first marriage*. This is the single most powerful predictor of marital stability. When half the women in America were married before age 20, you could predict that a lot of them would not have made a wise choice or have been mature enough to handle marriage and early motherhood. By the late 1960s, for many, that home in the suburbs seemed as confining as it had seemed liberating in the late 1940s. Among men who had married in the postwar years and who were upwardly mobile, many found that the young woman they had married out of high school did not fit their new lifestyle.

Other risk factors for divorce include low income and education, premarital pregnancy, husband's unemployment, and frequent residential moves (Shelton and Deen 2001). In general, employed wives are more likely than the unemployed wives to leave an unsatisfying marriage. Conversely, factors tending to preserve the marriage include participation in religious services and later age at first marriage, which is associated with shared decision making, planned pregnancies, adequate income, and emotional maturity.

Once married, the most powerful predictor of continued stability is, quite simply, the number of years already married. As is the case for most roles, the longer you stay, the more of your self is invested in the role's success and the harder it is to walk away and admit that you have wasted all that time. Most divorces occur very early in the marriage, in the first five years, and contrary to popular belief, there is no second peak when the children have left home; rates decline steadily with the length of the marriage. The presence of children does not appear to hold a troubled marriage together, although having a son attaches a father more closely to the family than does the presence a daughter (P. Schwartz 1994).

The American divorce rate is somewhat higher than that for other modern societies, but so, too, is our marriage rate, and, as you see in Figure 8.2, the two tend to move together. When assessing divorce rates, it should be kept in mind that, in the past, many marriages were terminated by the death of a spouse. It cannot be assumed, of course, that the couples who did not divorce in the past were happy in their marriage. Probably quite the opposite was true, but the costs of leaving the marriage were simply too great for women—instant poverty as well as a kind of social death in many communities.

Consequences. Although the social stigma has largely disappeared, the economic consequences of divorce for women remain strongly negative (Smock, Manning, and Gupta, 1999). About 15 percent of former wives are awarded *alimony,* and only half of them receive the full amount from their ex-husbands. There are also a few men who receive payments from an ex-wife. The dollar amounts of the awards averaged $5,000 a year in the late 1990s, which does not go a long way toward paying the rent.

Women with children may ask for *child support*, but only half the eligible mothers in 1997 were awarded anything, and only half of those collected the full amount, which, again, averaged only a few thousand dollars a year. When paid in full, however, child support can be crucial in lifting a family above the poverty line. At the same time, arguing over payments can escalate the existing conflict between parents. Many ex-husbands and fathers are themselves low-income earners, and many have a second family to support. Most give no material assistance to their children other than support payments. And although over half were given visitation rights, not all took advantage of the opportunity. It appears that for many children of divorce, their father becomes a shadowy figure (Garfinkel et al. 1998).

There are many negative outcomes of divorce for children, although it is difficult to separate the effects of divorce from those of the turmoil that preceded it (Hanson et al. 1998). For children living with their mother, the most common result is a loss of economic security, often requiring a change in residence that disrupts friendships and schooling. If the mother is a full-time employee, adequate supervision becomes a problem, as does her ability to help with homework and monitor school performance. Compared with their peers in two-parent households, children living with only their mother are more likely to drop out of high school, get into trouble with the police, and have spells of unemployment in adulthood (McLanahan and Sandefur 1994). Women who spent part of their childhood in a single-parent home are more likely than other women to marry early, have a premarital pregnancy, and ultimately to experience divorce themselves (Wolfinger 1999). Many of these negative consequences also characterize children from intact families where the parents are continually fighting.

When the family income is adequate, when the custodial parent has satisfying work, and when the noncustodial parent is in frequent contact, the children do as well as most from two-parent households. But these are not the typical conditions for American children of divorce. In contrast, in most European countries, social welfare policies protect all types of families from poverty and isolation. It is not the end of the marriage as much as the lack of supportive services that makes divorce a social problem in the United States (Goode 1993).

Thus, although divorce is the solution to many problems, it creates others. There is little evidence that ending a marriage is taken lightly by the vast majority of unhappily married couples. Nonetheless, the hope of fulfillment through marriage remains strong, and most divorced men and women venture into the marriage market once again. 5

Remarriage

Because divorces usually take place early in a marriage, before children are present, most men and women will remarry, the men sooner and at a higher rate than the women. The older and better educated the divorced woman, the lower her chances of remarriage because the pool of eligibles—divorced, widowed, or never-married educated men—is not very large. Men seeking to remarry can dip into a larger pool, filled with younger and less educated women.

As in the case of first marriage, just being married benefits men in terms of physical and mental health, although not necessarily economically (Nock 1998). Women gain immediately in terms of financial security, with remarriage as the most important factor in raising a family out of poverty. In comparison with first marriages, however, the risk of failure is somewhat higher the second (or third) time around—not for any deep psychological reasons but because there are not as many people to choose from so that more compromises have to be made between your ideal and what is available. For example, a woman may decide that a much older husband is better than none at all. Or a man may marry an attractive woman with several children rather than someone less attractive with no children.

When divorced parents remarry, they create a **blended family** composed of her children, his, and perhaps theirs. Despite all the difficulties in adjusting to a stepparent and to one another, the children will gain the financial and care-giving advantages of a two-parent family (Morrison and Rituolo 2000). Compared with only a few decades ago, American children and their parents live in increasingly varied types of households.

Family and Household Diversity in Contemporary America

When Americans think of "the family," the image is of a nuclear household composed of two parents and their young children, with the husband as major breadwinner; against this ideal other family forms appear "deviant." In reality, as seen in Table 8.3, the traditional pattern accounts for only about 7 percent of all households. Children are as likely to be living in a household with dual earners as with a single parent. What you see is a range of household types that meet people's needs at various points in the life cycle or that are forced upon them by circumstances. In Census terms, a "family" is a unit composed of two or more persons related by blood, marriage, or adoption. A mother and child is a family; so is a childless couple or two brothers sharing living quarters. "Households," in contrast, can be composed of one person or unrelated individuals living together (Demo, Allan, and Fine 2000).

The married couple/no children category includes both older couples whose children have grown as well as younger marrieds with "dual incomes/no kids," or DINKs. Similarly, the single-person household category lumps together young never-married adults and elderly widows, as well as divorced persons of any age (most of whom will remarry and be replaced by the newly divorced). It is possible that at different points in your life, you will be a member of each of these types of household. 6

Table 8.3 U.S. Households, 1999 (By Percentage)

	1970	1999
Married couple, children, one earner	24%	7%
Married couple, children, dual earners	16	17.5
Married couple, no children under 18	30	28
Single parent	11	16.5
One person household	17	26
Two or more nonmarried persons	2	5

Source: U.S. Bureau of the Census, Series P-20-527, 2000e.

Distribution of Household Types

The distribution of household types will vary by race/ethnicity. For example, Asian-American households are most likely to have two earners and children; whites to be DINKs, Hispanic families to fit the traditional one-earner pattern; and blacks to have a single householder. In addition, immigrant households may include other relatives, both for cultural and economic reasons. As noted in chapter 6, however, by the second and third generations, acculturation will also affect family structure and relationships.

Peter J. Stein

When divorced families remarry they create a blended family composed of her children, his children, and perhaps theirs.

The interplay among race, ethnicity, social class, gender, and immigration status is illustrated by the experience of many Latino families. Despite the important educational and income differences between Puerto Rican, Chicano, and South American subgroups, the general pattern for the first generation is to retain fairly traditional family structures and processes. Compared to all American women, Hispanic fertility rates are high and labor force participation is low. A reliance on the extended kinship system ("familism") has often been linked to cultural factors, but a more sociological analysis views these characteristics as logical responses to residential and economic segregation (Roschelle 1999).

Immigration and the flow of generations have also challenged traditional family power dynamics, as children become Americanized through schooling and wives enter the labor force. For Puerto Rican men, especially, low-status employment can erode one's ability to control other family members. At the intersection of ethnic, generational, and racial stratification systems, the class and gender dynamics of contemporary Latino families are in the process of rapid change (Kivisto and Runblad 2000).

African-American Families

From slavery to current welfare policies, structural forces have shaped the formation and functioning of many African-American families (Franklin 1997; Paterson 1998). Residential segregation and employment discrimination have created pockets of extreme poverty in urban and rural areas alike, while negative stereotypes of black women drive welfare policies that further impoverish the lives of women and children. As a consequence, compared with other racial and ethnic subgroups, black Americans are more likely to postpone marriage or never marry; to experience divorce, separation, and desertion; and to forgo remarriage. Fewer than half of African-American households are composed of a married couple, compared to about 80 percent for both whites and Asian Americans, and 70 percent for Hispanic households. In addition, almost half of black family households are headed by a mother, in contrast to about 15 percent for white households.

The shortage of marriageable men in inner-city black communities has already been noted. Large numbers are periodically unemployed as jobs move out of cities and into residentially segregated suburbs. Others are victims or perpetrators of crimes, filling American prisons. Many join the armed forces. The most successful quickly move out of the neighborhood. Those who stay face innumerable difficulties in providing for and protecting their families.

Young black women are faced with a tough choice: to take whatever affection is offered, however fleeting, or do without and hope that something permanent will come along. Most will end up raising children on their own. The prevalence of female-headed households has led some critics to speak of a *matriarchal* family system, but these are not women with much power in society, or even in their own communities. Nor are the households always without a male presence—a relative or boyfriend. The more accurate description is **matrifocal**, or woman-centered. Female kin—whether real or honorary—help one another, care for children, and try to negotiate the agencies and authorities that regulate so much of their lives (Hill Collins 1990). Although often perceived as "deviant," the matrifocal family has survived two centuries of slavery, segregation, and discrimination in America. There is some doubt, however, if even the kinship network of grandmothers, mothers, sisters, daughters, and "aunts" can survive the current period of diminishing welfare services, deteriorating housing and schools, and crime-ridden streets.

At the opposite end of the spectrum, almost two-thirds of high-income black men and women are in long-term marriages. These families typically have two adult wage earners, similar to one another in terms of education and occupational status. In other words, the middle-class African-American marriage is likely to be more egalitarian than its white counterpart because the partners are themselves more equal in status characteristics. In this sense, the black middle class marriage may be the pattern for all college-educated couples in the future. An alternative scenario notes that the wife's labor force participation is necessary to maintain middle-class status because wage and job discrimination have lowered the husband's earning power. It takes two wage earners to equal one white male's salary at the same level of education and skill (Toliver 1998).

In the middle, and often overlooked, are the majority of African-American households, firmly rooted in the working class (Horton et al. 2000). Family patterns among working-class blacks appear to be little different from their white educational and occupational peers, even though wages are typically lower.

Cohabitors

The word **cohabit** means to "live with." While cohabitors account for about 5 percent of American households today, 40 percent of Americans will have cohabited at some point over the life course. In 1999, the Census counted slightly over five million "persons of the opposite sex sharing living quarters" or POSSLQs ("possel-kews")—up from 1.5 million in 1980. Although one tends to think of cohabitors as being college-aged, most are over age 25, with only a high school education. It is estimated that close to half of American children will spend some part of their childhood living with one parent and her or his live-in partner (Smock 2000).

Are cohabitors different from couples who marry? Most will eventually marry, but many will not. Given the dramatic increase in age at first marriage, the availability of contraceptives, and greater public tolerance, it is probably too much to expect that all those young people will remain virginal until marriage. In the meantime they share living quarters for relatively short periods of time. The one characteristic that distinguishes younger cohabitors from noncohabitors is *religiosity*. The more religious the young person, the less likely he or she is to engage in premarital sex (Thornton 1992).

Does cohabitation have an effect on subsequent marriage? There are indications that divorce rates are higher for cohabitors who subsequently marry one another, but it is not clear what this means. People who cohabit may simply be less inclined than others to remain in an unhappy marriage. Many of the cohabitors are themselves divorced and unlikely to remarry, an effect that carries over to their children, who have lower marriage rates than children from intact families (Smock 2000). 7

Domestic Partnerships

Not all cohabitors are heterosexual. Some small percentage of nonmarried-couple households will be composed of lesbian or gay male partners. Contrary to popular beliefs, homosexual couples do *not* usually recreate the stereotyped heterosexual pattern of dominant male and submissive female. Rather, because the couple tends to be very similar in educational and occupational statuses, homosexual relationships are typically characterized by mutuality and equality (Sullivan 1996). The educational and income levels of homosexual Americans tend to be higher than the American average, and high proportions have been in relatively long-term relations, at least as long as many heterosexual unions (Black et al. 1999).

J.R. Halvorsen and G.E. Cisneros

A gay couple, living as domestic partners, celebrate their commitment to each other following a "holy union," a marriage-like ceremony, in a Protestant church.

In addition, many gay and lesbian couples have children from an earlier heterosexual relationship, adoption, or *in vitro* fertilization. As for the potential problems in raising children, the research on lesbian and gay male parenting has found "no differences on any measures between the heterosexual and homosexual parents regarding parenting styles, emotional adjustment, and sexual orientation of the children" (Allen and Burrell 1996, 19).

If couples could be evaluated on the basis of the quality of their commitment and depth of caring, rather than by the sex of partners, many homosexual unions would be judged healthier (or at least less destructive) than some heterosexual marriages. Conversely, there are violent and exploitive gay relationships, just as there are among heterosexuals. The great difficulty for a gay person is that as much as he or she may long for a lasting relationship, the pool of potential partners is so small that success becomes much more problematic than for heterosexuals.

Nonetheless, the idea of acknowledging the validity of marriage-like unions between people of the same sex is no longer as far-fetched as only a decade ago. Increasingly, businesses, local governments, and academic institutions are recognizing the rights of **domestic partners**, people who live together in a committed relationship, to be covered by the same benefits as married employees. The French government, in 1999, recognized a "civil pact of solidarity" by which a homosexual couple is officially registered as responsible for one another and entitled to the same treatment as their heterosexual married peers. As with a marriage, the civil pact can be terminated by another official process.

In North America, an 8–1 decision by the Supreme Court of Canada in mid-1999 struck down the law that defined "spouse" as applying only to heterosexuals. This decision opened the way for widespread changes in federal statutes to eliminate any differences in the legal standing of heterosexuals and homosexuals (*New York Times,* May 21, 1999). It is expected that most Canadian provinces will also amend their laws.

Across the border, in December 1999, the Supreme Court of Vermont ruled unanimously that the state must extend the same benefits to gay and lesbian couples that are afforded to heterosexual spouses. To ensure that such legal protections are provided, the Court gave the state legislature the choice of recognizing gay marriage or enacting the most sweeping domestic partnership law in the nation (Goldberg 1999). The legislature responded in mid-2000 with a domestic partnership law that could eventually be a model for other states. 8

It is unlikely that other states will follow soon. Under enormous pressure from religious and political conservatives, back in 1996 when it appeared that the Supreme Court of Hawaii might sanction same-sex unions, a majority of state legislatures proposed laws to bar homosexual marriages and deny recognition to those performed in any other state. There may be a constitutional difficulty here, as one of the basic underpinnings of the U.S. system is the "full faith and credit" clause that mandates recognition of marriages and divorces from one state to another. To deal with this problem, Congress passed the Defense of Marriage Act of 1996 that releases the states and other territories of the United States from an obligation to recognize same-sex marriages under the laws of another state. The Act will ultimately be challenged in the U.S. Supreme Court. 9

Single-Parent Households

As a result of divorce and nonmarital childbearing, only 68 percent of children under 18 years old live with both parents today, compared with 77 percent in 1980. Twenty-three percent live with their mother, 4 percent with their father, and another 4 percent with neither parent. While 75 percent of white children live with both parents, this is true for only 36 percent of black youngsters. The Census data, however, obscure the extent to which there may be a cohabitating adult in the household. It is estimated that 40 percent of the children born to unmarried mothers are raised in homes with two adults, at least for part of the time (Bumpass and Lu 2000).

As noted earlier in this chapter, the major problem for the single-mother family is lack of money. Not all single mothers are equal; much depends on whether the mother is widowed, divorced, or never married, largely because each has different economic consequences. The less financially secure the household, the more problematic the outcomes for children in terms of education, occupational status, and personal happiness in adulthood (Biblarz and Gottainer 2000). In general, widowed mothers are more financially secure than divorced mothers, and the divorced are better off than the never married.

Over half of children in mother-only families live below the poverty level, compared to 10 percent in two-parent households. The 1996 law that ended federal welfare payments makes it even harder for the mother to count on steady income. The jobs available to her often pay less than the poverty level, while state agencies have made it difficult to receive health and other benefits. Finding adequate child care is extremely difficult, even for women with money.

At the other end of the single-mother spectrum are the Murphy Browns—white, middle-class, college-educated women who choose to bear and raise children without the benefit of marriage. For these women, who have chosen motherhood and who are financially secure, the link between marriage and maternity has become optional.

Today, about 20 percent of single-parent households are headed by a father, double the proportion in 1980. Compared to single mothers, the fathers tend to have higher incomes, to have household help, and to remarry within a few years. How do they behave in the parent role? Just like a mother (Risman et al. 1999). It is not the sex of the parent but the demands of the situation that shape feelings and actions. Balancing home and work responsibilities, for both single-parent fathers and mothers, is greatly aided by supportive employers and coworkers. 10

Dual-Earner Families

Today, a majority of two-parent households also have two employed adults. Seventy-two percent of married mothers are in the labor force, including 77 percent of those with children between ages 7 and 16, and 64 percent of mothers of children age 6 and under.

It is the two incomes that lift some families out of poverty and that keep others firmly planted in the middle class. With the exception of men in the top occupational brackets, the family income for dual-earner households is double that of single earners at similar skill levels. This fact alone makes it unlikely that women will leave the labor force in large numbers any time soon. In addition to the independence gained by earning one's own money, employed women also derive benefits in self-esteem and the friendship network of colleagues (Prather 2000). Indeed, the trend is toward an increasingly earlier return to work after childbirth, for all these reasons in addition to ensuring continued health benefits (Orenstein 2000). For some working women, however, low pay and low job satisfaction, combined with full responsibility for housework and child care, can erase the benefits of employment (Spade 1994). For others, when domestic chores seem endless and unsatisfying, paid work can be a less demanding and more rewarding refuge (Hochschild 1997).

There is little evidence that children are harmed by a mother's labor force participation and much to indicate that her sense of well-being plus the added income are beneficial to the children, especially if she has help with household chores (Chira 1998; Deutsch 1999). Recent research also suggests that the image of a generation of "latchkey" children is vastly overdrawn. Only 12 to 14 percent of children aged 5 to 12 spend any time on their own at home between the end of school and the arrival of a parent; the average time

Box 8.1

Daddy's in the Kitchen: The New Division of Family Labor

The key to success for dual-earner couples is a division of labor that both partners consider fair. It does not have to be equal, just perceived as fair enough to relieve a working mother of constant worry and role overload, but not so much as to cause a father's resentment. Data on men's contributions to homemaking and child care are difficult to interpret because as the wife/mother reduces the time she spends on these tasks, his share of the total will rise for the same number of hours. In addition, the division of household labor tends to be gender-typed: The outside is his, the inside hers, which is why the garbage is such a bone of contention—it is generated inside but gets disposed of outside.

The area of greatest change is men's involvement in child care. However, a number of barriers remain. One problem for many men is the ridicule they face from employers and coworkers. You can imagine the reaction to a colleague who said he was leaving early to take his daughter to dancing class. In addition, most workplaces are not flexible enough to allow employees to come and go at different times. Men on an upward career path take great risks when they appear to value family responsibilities over loyalty to the firm.

Unlike many European countries, the United States does not a have a program that provides income and social services to workers who need to take time off to care for a newborn or ill child, spouse, or elderly parent. The U.S. Family Leave Act of 1993, which covers less than 30 percent of the labor force, only says that you can not be fired or lose a promotion or benefits because you chose to take *unpaid* time off to care for a newborn or ailing family member. As a result, very few women and even fewer men have taken advantage of the opportunity.

Despite these barriers, it does appear that married men are spending more time with their children than did their own fathers, beginning with the birth itself (Levine 2000). For one-fifth of preschool children, their father is the main caregiver while mommy is at work, either because the couple works split shifts or because he can work at home. An additional 8 to 10 percent of men are not looking for work because of "home responsibilities"—up from 4.6 percent in 1991. And a national organization of "At-Home Dads" now runs its own website. Clearly, the division of household labor is more varied than in the past, and the long-term benefits of a nurturing father for the emotional development of daughters and sons are increasingly apparent (Warner and Steel 1999).

Box 8.2

Who Cares?

Caring work is typically assigned to women in their role as nurturer. When performed in the home by family members, care giving remains invisible and devalued in a society where only paid work counts as real (Glenn 2000). The woman's reward is praise for selfless devotion. Yet daughters and wives relieve men of the burden of domestic labor. When care giving is performed by hired help it is devalued even further. Home health aides are among the lowest paid, least honored members of the labor force (Cancian and Oliker 2000).

Upper-income and dual-earner households that depend on paid domestic workers have produced a three-teired division of labor (Parrenas 2000). At the top is the woman who hires the maid, home health aide, or nanny; then there is the woman being hired, who needs the money to support her own family; and, finally, the even poorer woman who takes care of the paid worker's children. In many cases, the hired worker comes from abroad, such as Philippina maids, West Indian health aides, and British nannies—a global chain of care giving (Hochschild 2000).

If care giving is such a virtuous activity, why is it so hidden and poorly rewarded?

spent alone is one hour. Most of these are older children, many of whom value their "down time" alone (Hofferth and Jankuniene 2000).

The effects of a wife's employment on her husband's well-being are complex (Coltrane and Adams 2001). Many men are relieved at sharing economic responsibilities and having the added income. Others feel emasculated, and some even lower their share of housework. Not surprisingly, then, divorce rates are higher for dual-earner than for single-earner couples, but this higher rate could simply reflect an employed woman's greater ability to leave an unhappy marriage. Nonetheless, working out compatible schedules and learning to share breadwinning and home and child-care tasks will be a major challenge for all but a few American couples in the future (Deutsch 1999).

Variations on the dual-earner model include: (1) **Dual-career couples**—careers differ from a job in requiring a deeper commitment of time and energy, but the pay-off is a higher salary. Thus, while the difficulties of a dual-earner family are magnified by the demands of a career, the added income can buy a lot of services. (2) **Commuter marriages**—there are career opportunities that require a couple to live in different places, working apart during the week and spending weekends and long vacations together (Gerstel 1999). Some marriages thrive when the partners are not together all the time, but it is difficult when children are involved. As a result, commuter arrangements are most common among couples who choose to remain childless or whose children have left the nest. 11

The New Family Cycle

The convergence of many of the trends covered in this chapter—age at marriage, mate selection, divorce, and remarriage—plus those covered in other chapters, such as increased life expectancy (chapter 15), greater independence for women (chapter 7), and reproductive choices (chapter 4), have created a "modern family life cycle" different from that of even a generation ago. 12

1. At the beginning of the cycle, there is the decade or more between sexual maturity and marriage, during which young people experiment with intimacy and narrow down the pool of eligibles.
2. Once married, the couple typically has two children born within a few years of one another, so that even with later age at marriage, childbearing is completed by the time the mother is in her mid-thirties.
3. The children begin to leave home while the parents are still relatively young, creating a new phase in the life course: *the empty nest*. For couples who have survived all the difficulties of child rearing, satisfaction in marriage at this phase rises to the level of the newlywed stage.
4. Because middle-aged Americans today can expect to live well into their 80s, the nest stays empty for quite a while—except for periods of housing a "boomerang baby," a grown child who returns to the nest for refueling. Can you figure out why sons are far more likely than daughters to come home for months at a time? The middle-aged wife or mother, however, must also cope with aging parents. Despite all the changes in her life, she is still the one expected to do all the "kinkeeping," not only for her parents but for her husband's as well.
5. The added years bring widowhood to most women, due to higher death rates for men plus the fact that husbands are typically older than their wives.

Thus, the family life cycle ends where it began, with a single-person household.

Although children will have fewer siblings and may live with only one parent for part of their growing up, they will know more of their grandparents and even great-grandparents and spend more time with them than in the past. If you think about it, a child whose parents divorce and remarry could have four or more sets of grandparents. It is not uncommon today for grandparents to continue to stay in touch with grandchildren even after the parents have split.

In some cases, the grandparents take over the parent role. In the late 1990s, close to 4 million children were living in homes maintained by a grandparent—double the proportion in 1970 (Bryson and Casper 1999). Grandparents also provide about 16 percent of child care for working mothers, either in their own home or in that of the child.

What is most striking about contemporary families is their great diversity. Critics and politicians who call for a return to "traditional family values" are idealizing what was a temporary adaptation to historical conditions (Coontz 1997). It is doubtful that many of you would willingly return to an extended family system in which your needs would be sacrificed to those of the kinship group. Since there are no laws against multigenerational living, we assume that the spread of nuclear households is evidence that married couples do not want to live with their parents or other relatives. And since women are not being forced to wait for marriage or to have only two children or to enter the labor force, it seems likely that these decisions represent their wishes (Demo, Allen, and Fine 2000).

The diversity of family structures today appears to be an adaptive response to the postmodern world: to changing needs across the life course, extended life expectancy, the decline of patriarchy, the emancipation of women and children, and, above all, the emphasis on self-fulfillment and the privacy of intimate relationships (Gerson 2000). For many, the choice may be between the "new family" of egalitarian flexibility or "no family," by forgoing marriage and/or parenthood (Goldscheider and Waite 1991). But short of forcing couples to stay together, there really is not any viable alternative to letting them dissolve a miserable union. Nevertheless, much could be done to strengthen families through public programs that provide income supports for all households with children, day-care facilities for preschoolers and the frail elderly, paid family leave, housing assistance, and counseling services.

The downside to the modern emphasis on individual happiness is that you can become so self-centered that you forget your responsibilities to others and the community at large. The most difficult task of your adulthood will be to find a balance between the demands of self and others. The good news is that both women and men can choose among a range of family forms in order to realize Freud's formula for the good life: To be fulfilled in love and work.

Conclusion

This chapter has examined the family as a social construction across cultures and through history. You have seen how the modern family differs from the traditional types, in both form and function. The contemporary nuclear family is specialized for the early socialization of children and the emotional well-being of all members. You are essentially on your own in choosing your life partner(s) and establishing a supportive environment for personal growth, and while the failure rate is high, so are the rewards of success. Modern conditions have led to a diversity of households, with or without children or marriage. The chapter closed with a description of the changing family life cycle.

Surfing the Sociological Internet

1 Kinship: **http://daphne.palomar.edu/kinship/**

2 Family Resources:
http://osiris.colorado.edu/SOC/RES/family.html
http://www.familydiscussions.com/
http://www.aacap.org/publications/factsfam/index.htm
http://www.nimh.nih.gov/publicat/baschap6.cfm#marr

3 Household Statistics: **http://www.census.gov/**
Latino Families: **http://www.elclick.com/**
Asian-American Families: **http://www.cacf.org/**
African-American Families:
http://www.blackfamilies.com
http://www.blackparenting.com/main.shtml

4 Family Violence:
http://www.famvi.com/
http://www.silcom.com/~paladin/madv/

5 Divorce: **http://www.divorcenet.com/**
Children and divorce:
http://www.muextension.missouri.edu/xplor/hesguide/humanrel/gh6600.htm

6 Worldwide summary on domestic partnerships, cohabiting, and marriage:
http://www.iglhrc.org/news/faqs/marriage_981103.html

7 Cohabiting: **http://hometown.aol.com/cohabiting**

8 Domestic Partnerships:
http://208.178.40.104/cgi-bin/pages/issues/record?record=3
http://www.aclu.org/issues/gay/dpmodel.html

9 To see locate the full text of the Defense of Marriage Act, go to:
http://thomas.loc.gov/

10 Resources for single parents:
http://www.singlemoms.org/
http://single-parents.somewhere.net/

11 Working Families Resources—Dual earner and dual career couples:
http://workingfamilies.berkeley.edu/
http://www.spc.uchicago.edu/orgs/sloan/papers.html

12 The Family Life Cycle: **http://www.blcc.cornell.edu/**

Glossary

Blended Family Unit created when divorced parents remarry and are joined by her children and his children.
Cohabitation Nonmarried persons sharing living quarters.
Commuter Marriages A couple whose career opportunities require them to live in different places.
Domestic Partners Persons who live together in a committed relationship recognized by the state.
Dual Career Couples Both partners have a career.
Dual Earner Families Both partners are in the labor force.
Egalitarianism The reduction of power differences between husband and wife and between parents and children.
Extended Family A unit composed of related households (often involving three or more generations) sharing economic tasks and providing support in illness and old age.
Family System A society's set of rules and roles that govern mate selection and marriage.
Heterogamy The tendency to select a marriage partner of a different race, religion, ethnicity, or social class.

Homogamy The tendency to select a marriage partner who shares your characteristics, such as race, religion, ethnicity, and social class.
Incest Taboos Rules that forbid sexual relations among blood relatives.
Matrifocal Families centered on the woman.
Nuclear Family A unit composed of a married couple and their dependent children.
Principle of Legitimacy (social fatherhood) Principle holding one man, the husband, responsible for his wife's children, whether or not he is their biological father.
Rule of Reciprocity Principle of social life dictating that if a gift is received, the receiver is obligated to return something of equal value. ✦

Chapter Eight: Additional Readings

Narrative Essay

THEY LIVE THE DREAM

by Dan Rather

It is the phrase we reach for most often to describe this land of ours. It has reflected what is best in us as a county and a people. It is the American Dream, and it has filled me with awe for as long as I can remember.

Growing up in Houston during the Great Depression, it took shape for me around the radio, as I listened spellbound to Edward R. Murrow's World War II dispatches and dreamed of becoming a reporter myself. My neighborhood was not a place that led me to think I should be reaching for such a far away star. Yet—and this still gives me a thrill today—within 20 years, there I was, a correspondent in New York City meeting Murrow, my childhood hero.

The American Dream, you see, holds me in its grasp because I have been blessed to live my own version of it. There is no typical American and typical American Dream. For some, the dream is freedom; for others, it is of fortune or family or service to one's fellows. Some place great emphasis on the pursuit of happiness or of keeping alive the innovative spirit. But however we define it, it defines us as a people.

The people you'll meet here are the result of my quest to discover the American Dream as your neighbors are creating it today. I think you will find them inspirational. I know I did.

DELORES KESLER: *SHE STARTED HER COMPANY JUST TO SURVIVE AND RETIRED A MILLIONAIRE.*

Delores Kesler's dream began with a $10,000 loan she used to found a temporary staffing agency in Jacksonville, Florida in 1977. When she retired 20 years later, her company, AccuStaff, had projected revenues of $2 billion. Kesler says she didn't plan to become a millionaire: Divorced and with a small child, she began her career at 22 with a series of dead-end jobs, struggling to make ends meet. When she founded her company, there were few women entrepreneurs. But her father had often told Kesler she could do anything she wanted to do, and she was determined to succeed. As time went on, however, Kesler realized it was not just financial gain she was pursuing: She wanted to make a contribution to her community. And, as her business grew, she started requiring her employees to devote time to community service and insisting that her company contribute to local charities. And she didn't stop there. In time, Kesler's company was earning $50 million a year, and a large portion was going back into the community. When Kesler retired, she set a new course for her life. Today, the Delores Pass Kesler Foundation focuses on changing young lives through education, mentoring and children's programs. In 1997, she gave $1 million to the University of North Florida to provide scholarships to students from Rains High School in Jacksonville. She cried before an audience of thousands when the principal thanked her. She told them that they didn't know how good it felt to be able to give that money away. "An awful lot of people benefited from what started with a $10,000 loan," Kesler says.

WAYNE WARD FORD: *A TROUBLED YOUNG MAN, HE HAD AN ODD PREMONITION ABOUT HIS FUTURE.*

Wayne Ford was in eighth grade when a teacher asked the class to write their obituaries. How would they like to be remembered? Ford, who lived in a rough area of Washington, D.C., came up with a curious response: He said he would make his mark in the Mid-West. He would be active in politics and in charge of a community center.

Wayne Ford would go on to get in trouble in high school. "I was doing drugs, robbing, breaking into apartments," he recalls. To get away, he accepted a football scholarship to a small, nearly all-white Minnesota college. Once there, however, racism threatened to throw him off course. Instead, he turned his anger to activism and founded the school's black student union.

"Then," he says, "it all started to come together. The worst things in my life were the things that had the potential to make me great." Ford devoted himself to academics. History especially gave him a new perspective. "When I started reading it," he says, "I thought, 'My God, the world has gone though hell, not just Wayne Ford.' "

After graduation, Ford turned to politics. Today, he's living the dream he had as a boy: He's the only black member of the Iowa State Legislature and the founder and executive director of Urban Dreams, a nonprofit community program for at-risk youth. Last year, he spoke before the Democratic National Convention. It was one of the biggest achievements of his life, but he says, "It wasn't the cherry on the ice cream. The best is yet to come."

SHAWN CARLSON: *His grandfather's struggle to be accepted inspired him to encourage others.*

Shawn Carlson says his dream and his passion—the Society for Amateur Scientists, which he founded—was inspired by his grandfather. "I've been privileged to know some of the greatest scientists alive today," says Carlson, who has a Ph.D. in nuclear physics. "And no one had a greater raw scientific talent than my grandfather." But, he adds, his grandfather's work was consistently rejected "because he didn't have the letters 'Ph.D.' next to his name."

"Amateur scientists," he says, "are overflowing with passion," and his aim is to teach them standards and procedures so the larger scientific world will take them seriously. He and his wife, Michelle, sank their life savings of $10,000 into starting the Society for Amateur Scientists in 1994 and endured several tough years. Then Carlson was awarded a MacArthur "genius" fellowship, which allowed him to keep the Society afloat.

Although he has been criticized by some in the scientific community, Carlson continues to pursue his dream of opening scientific innovation to everyone. "The ability to come up with something original and be respected because you are a maverick—that's very much part of the American tradition," he says.

OSCAR CARLOS ACOSTA: *Everything he wanted was within his grasp. Then, it seemed, it was gone.*

As a boy in tiny Elida, NM, Oscar Acosta had a talent for throwing a baseball that brought him a college scholarship and a chance at athletic glory. Getting to the Majors was his dream, and he neglected everything else—his schoolwork and his wife and children—to get there. "I became consumed," he says. He made it to the minor leagues, but when a torn rotator cuff ended his pitching career, his life spiraled out of control. His wife took the kids and left. He was broke. He lost any belief in himself. "I'd just given up," he says. "I thought I was destined to go back and be a cow-puncher the rest of my life."

When he got a second chance—an offer to coach in the Texas Rangers' minor league system—Acosta says, he realized it was time to change. His identity, he swore, would never be tied exclusively to baseball. He reconciled with his wife and for the next 11 years built back what he'd lost, taking his blessings as they came. "I told my daughter, if God wants me to be a minor league instructor, that's what I'm going to do," he says.

Acosta did make it to the majors—as a pitching coach for the Chicago Cubs. Now 44, he lives not far from where he grew up. Recently, Acosta watched his son play in a little League game on the same field where he'd learned to pitch. "This was a big deal," Acosta says. "It was like watching myself—like my life had started all over."

EILEEN COLLINS: *SHE FOUND WHAT SHE WANTED TO DO IN LIFE, BUT HOW IN THE WORLD WOULD SHE GET THERE?*

The first woman to pilot the Space Shuttle and to command a Shuttle mission grew up in public housing in Elmira, NY. There wasn't much money for family outings when she was a child. "One thing my father liked to do," recalls Eileen Collins, "was take us to the airport to watch the planes take off." She knew she wanted to fly, so Collins saved up for lessons, and she had enough by the time she attended community college. Once in the pilot's seat, her future seemed clear: "You know how you find the thing that you like to do in life?" she says. "I found it."

Collins pursued her dream, joining Air Force ROTC at Syracuse University and being among the first women allowed into the pilot-training program. But she didn't stop there. Eventually, she set her sights even higher—on NASA.

She recalls an early look out the window of the Shuttle: "Looking back at Earth is just beautiful. It's blue, it's white, it's tan. The jungles are a dark green. There's so much water. It's just amazing." And when Collins got the opportunity to land the Shuttle—the first woman to do so—she says, "I knew all those women pilots out there were watching me and thinking, 'Eileen, you better make a good landing.' " She did.

"I'm an explorer," says Collins, now 44. "I want to go places that are new and different, learn new things. I think that's what being human is all about. It's what life is all about—exploring and learning."

You may see a common thread running though many of these stories. The American Dream affords us opportunity and the freedom to seize it. It has also created, in my experience, some of the most generous people in the world. Americans who find their own dream make the dreams of their fellow citizens possible as well. For them, and for the rest of us, the Dream remains both a hope and a promise, even as we add to its meaning with each new chapter of our lives.

Narrative Essay

Me and My Shadow

by Cathy Anne Murtha

"Paws for Independence" is the motto of Southeastern Guide Dogs of Central Florida. These words carry special meaning for me. They signify the freedom and sense of independence that I now hold within my heart and exhibit on a daily basis through the assistance and companionship of my best friend, my guide dog, Shadow. Meeting Shadow in the living room of Southeastern Guide Dogs was one of the most memorable moments of my life. The frisky little black Lab that leapt into my arms three years ago has become an invaluable friend to me. When we first met, I could not imagine how that little bundle of energy could possibly settle down into a competent working dog. She managed to push all my fears aside the first time I took the leather handle of her harness in my hand. Shadow, four years old, has continued to amaze me throughout our two years of working together. We are best friends and constant companions.

The sense of excitement in the spacious living room of Southeastern Guide Dogs was palpable on that sultry August day in 1993. Twelve blind students from all walks of life and all regions of the United States were about to experience great change. We were not to understand the special bond that would be created or how much pleasure we would derive from these incredible animals until much later. At that moment, all we could feel was a sense of overwhelming anticipation.

One by one the dogs were brought into the room. We could hear the toenails skittering on the linoleum of the hall as the trainers struggled to control the dogs' excitement. It was hard to believe, but it was very possible—they were almost more excited than we were. The trainers tried valiantly to maintain a sense of dignity about the occasion; however, as more dogs entered the room, the party atmosphere overwhelmed one and all. Wet noses were thrust into our surprised faces, greetings and doggy kisses were offered by the four-legged bundles of energy, and happy tails thwapped our faces. Laughter spread throughout the room. Golden Retrievers, smooth-coated Collies, and German Shepherds dragged their trainers into the room. As the trainers handed the leashes to the appropriate students, the greetings began. The dogs really didn't care whom they were saying "hi" to; it seemed like everyone was catching a wet tongue on his face or having the air whooshed from his lungs by an eager pup who wanted to be the center of attention.

I sat on the sofa, listening to the excitement, remembering a similar moment seven years previous when I had received my first guide dog, a rambunctious black lab named Coral. I remembered the sense of awe and wonder that filled me. I felt that feeling returning. I listened for my name to be called. Because I was a returning graduate, I had a feeling I would be one of the last to receive my dog. My heart was beating faster as I waited, trying to be patient, trying to control the sense of excitement that would not be quelled. Finally, I heard my name announced. I heard the words "Black Labrador" and a name . . . "Shadow." Suddenly there was a cold nose on my hand, a velvet ear, a sleek black body and a ferociously waving tail. Two paws were planted firmly in my lap; Shadow and I were nose to nose. She sniffed me gently; I felt my hands wrap around her strong neck; I held her close. I murmured her beautiful name over and over again, "Shadow." Tears welled in my eyes. I had missed having a dog in my life since having to retire Coral. Coral had developed epilepsy and had gone to live with a good friend of mine. I wondered if I would be able to enjoy more years with Shadow. I felt trepidation creep over me, but I thrust it aside! I let the tears fall and decided that Shadow was mine; we would be together for a very long time!

Just as a mother checks on a newborn baby, later that night I found myself creeping to the bottom of my bed, reaching over to feel my dog. I would usually be met with a moist nose and the happy thump of Shadow's tail against the floor. I am not sure, to this day, why I felt that need to check on her. Perhaps I wanted to be sure she was real, or that she was okay, or that she was really there. I only know that I felt a sense of wonder and satisfaction each time she was there, breathing softly and curled in her customary little ball.

The next day the other students and I assembled in the sun porch and waited for our turn to work our dogs for the first time in harness. I decided not to anticipate my moment, but to enjoy those of my companions. One by one they left the sun porch; I could feel their sense of doubt; many had come to the school expecting something but had no real concept of what a guide dog could do. They had gone through the interviews, had many meetings during the previous three days, but this was the moment that would tell them that their lives were about to change. They left the porch not knowing what to expect; they were hopeful, but the skepticism was in their voices and actions. At that moment, their companions were just dogs—wonderful, frisky creatures—but they had no concept of the miraculous changes that would take place when the harnesses were snapped beneath their dogs' chests. It was not possible to convey the experience to students who had not yet worked their dogs; words like incredible, wonderful, and freedom tumbled out. Freedom, the word hung in the air; I felt it swirling through my mind when I was called to bring Shadow to the work area. I rose from my chair. Shadow heeled perfectly. My head was in a daze; my fingers caressed the soft leather of the harness that was slung over my shoulder. I wondered if our relationship would be as good as Coral's and mine. I had returned to cane travel three months before arriving at Southeastern. Now the moment had come to welcome a new companion into my life. I was afraid of making comparisons, afraid that I would not give Shadow a fair chance, afraid that I would be disappointed.

The harness slid over Shadow's wriggling head; as I buckled it into place, her nose touched my face; a gentle sniff was offered. I patted her gently on the head and ran my hand down the length of her body. Her tail was wagging, not with the enthusiasm of a puppy, but with self-assurance. When the chest strap was buckled into place, Shadow was transformed. She was a working Guide Dog and knew it! I stood beside her, the harness held loosely in my left hand, the leash looped through two fingers; I gave the command: "Forward!" Words cannot express what I experienced at that moment. I thought it would be the same as the first time I picked up Coral's harness, but it wasn't. It was so much more! Shadow strode out with confidence. I could feel the wind in my face and listen to the birds singing high in the trees. I felt the sun shining down on us as we strode down the sidewalk. I no longer worried about running off a curb or having to listen for pedestrians. I remember wondering if that was how a sighted person felt as he strode down the sidewalk. In that moment all the fears I had been trying to push aside left me. I silently apologized to Shadow for my doubts and began to talk to her. I told her what a good dog she was, how special she was, and what a wonderful job she was doing. I felt the first of many acknowledgments that were to follow. Shadow turned slightly and bumped her soft muzzle gently against my knee. This is a signal that Shadow continues to use today. If I am not talking enough, if I don't acknowledge an especially great aversion quickly enough, if I don't know that she has just walked around a gaping hole in the sidewalk and saved me from tumbling head-long into a chasm filled with jagged chunks of concrete, I will feel the familiar, gentle nudge and know that I have been negligent in my responsibilities.

Shadow has proven to be an exceptional working dog. This is not only due to the excellent training she received at Southeastern Guide Dogs, but also to the family that gave her the love and training she needed as a puppy. Shadow is secure in any environment. She handles even the most treacherous of obstacles with self-confidence and pride. She is a gentle and loving creature whose only desire is to please me and receive the acknowledgment she deserves. Meeting Shadow and welcoming her into my life was an experience that will never be repeated, but each time I pick up the harness and command her to go forward, I feel the Florida sun and hear birds. I remember our first walk and think of the word that best describes our relationship, the word that swam in my head on the humid August day—freedom.

Addendum

Shadow wears a sign that says, "Do Not Pet Me. I am a Southeastern Guide Dog." Since many are tempted to pet or embrace her, it is important to stress the rules about not petting guide dogs. Guide dogs in public should never receive attention of any kind, not even a "hello" without permission of the guide dog user. Petting, feeding, calling and approaching a guide dog should absolutely never be done. These are working dogs, trained to be attentive to their job, and they should not be distracted even with the kindest of intentions.

Narrative Essay

AIDS in Africa

by Raulyne Kenfack

Twenty years ago, the disease now known as the Acquired Immune Deficiency Syndrome (AIDS) was first recognized. AIDS represents a late stage of infection by a retrovirus called Human Immune Deficiency Virus (HIV) of which there are two types: HIV1 and HIV2. The first one is associated with the epidemic in Central, East, and Southern Africa, and the rest of the world. The second one has been associated with people from several West African countries. In Africa, low education, especially among women, is one of the many causes behind the epidemic.

In some African societies, a woman is relegated to a position of secondary importance. While the years pass by, her life remains under the authority of her husband or son: she has little or no say in decisions concerning her sexual life. If a woman suggests a condom, or avoids high-risk sexual behavior, she is immediately accused of adultery and promiscuity and suspected of having been infected with a Sexually Transmitted Disease (STD) by a man other than her husband. On the other hand, a man enjoys greater sexual freedom. It is acceptable for him to be sexually active; he can have more than one wife, and he can maintain many sexual relationships. In most African cultures, there is a code that has allowed and encouraged a man to have more than one wife. Therefore, the woman's inferior position regarding the couple's sexual life added to poverty does not permit dialogue about STDs and AIDS.

More than two-thirds of the families in Africa live on less than two dollars a day. Most families don't even have enough money to pay for their children's first step of education in elementary school. The new protease inhibitors, necessary to turn AIDS from a death path to a chronic disease, cost at least $12,000 per person each year. The average African nation spends less than $10 per person each year on health care. It is not uncommon to have more than ten people living in a three-bedroom house with a tiny income. Poorer families have a greater tendency to die from AIDS than do richer ones for very obvious reasons. In poverty, there are no money savings or other assets to bring relief to the impact of illnesses. Of the global total of 30 million people living with HIV worldwide, about two-thirds are in sub-Sahara Africa. It is estimated that of the 12 million people who have died from HIV-related illnesses since the start of the epidemic worldwide, about 9 million have been Africans. Those who are poor in Africa and are infected with HIV live for a shorter time than those in developed countries. With those conditions helping the spread of the disease in Africa, a small group of professional women met in Stockholm, Sweden, in June 1988, and created the Society for Women and AIDS in Africa (SWAA). The women were concerned with the growing incidences of HIV infection, particularly in women and children.

In 1994, the SWAA needed to reach the heart of the uninformed population. And because the SWAA didn't have enough money or resources to do so, the organization asked for help. I volunteered for a campaign of information for one month in a village named Tsinkop, located in Cameroon, West Africa. My task was to make the villagers realize that AIDS existed, and to convince them to use the simplest protection available—which is the use of a condom. Even though the inhabitants of that village were dying of AIDS, they were still in denial. The villagers believed it was a malediction from the gods. Because the villagers hadn't made enough sacrifices to their ancestors, the gods were angry. According to their traditional or cultural belief, the villagers—after every happy or sad moment—had to share most of their belongings by putting them next to huge waterfalls of the village to honor their gods and ancestors, or to seek some answers to questions from them. The waterfalls were supposed to have some sort of connection with the gods and the village's sorcerer. Everybody was very anxious as they waited three days before the sorcerer came out of his meditation and encounters with the sprits to announce that the gods only told him there would be more death! This type of practice to seek some answers is often used in Africa. Anyway, I couldn't wait to get my mission started, and to give them answers they didn't have from the gods.

I started by showing every villager pictures of men, women, and children who had died from AIDS in the cities. These people had died in ways similar to how villagers had died. As I said before, AIDS has emerged as another disease of disadvantage and deprivation linked to social factors such as poverty, social status, and urbanization. After showing the inhabitants of that village pictures, I first talked to the men because they didn't want their wives to learn anything from the western world; in many rural areas in Africa, people are very conservative. They consider everything coming from the outside as sacrilegious or ominous. They are especially suspicious of, as they said, "white civilizations where women are involved with everything." Some of them even told me that they didn't want me to "modernize their wives!" Their restrictions with the outside world made it even harder for me to lay down some explanations about the disease. As I mentioned before, men in Tsinkop like to be very sexually active; therefore, I knew that their biggest concern was my putting a brake in their sexual lives. After showing them pictures, I started to explain how the disease is contracted sexually.

I knew deeply that something had to be done; I had to get those men concerned one way or another. At that particular moment, I decided to have a meeting with the women behind their husbands' backs. It was not very fair to them, but I felt it necessary to do something in order to save that small village. What gave me enough courage was the look on those women's faces; they were desperate for a solution, and they didn't want to bury any more relatives. Every day for two weeks, while the women were working, we talked about their sexuality related to the disease. I taught them different ways to get protection, but what mattered the most was to communicate with their mates and to reach their hearts and souls. At first the men were very reticent; some men even threatened to get a divorce if they had to wear protection to have sex. In other ways, a small number of men were very favorable to the situation. I had already spent two weeks there and the outcome was not remarkable.

Then I realized that the village's sorcerer was the man everybody would listen to since he is considered the representative of the gods in the village. I spoke to him for more than an hour and answered many questions from him, trying to convince him about the power of the deadly virus. At the end of the conversation, his only reaction was "I will give you an answer tomorrow." I never knew what happened that night; I guess he consulted the spirits. Nevertheless, early the following morning, he gathered the entire village and asked everybody to follow my advice without objection. I was thrilled and once again explained step by step what I knew about AIDS. The SWAA was providing the simplest protection for the men in the village: condoms for every man, with the help of a small hospital nearby. After one month of counseling, everybody in the village agreed to fight against the disease.

Scientists are still working to find a vaccine. With a true partnership, in the form of a grand coalition of leaders, organizations and individuals at any level, everybody is working in different ways towards the common goal: the conquest of HIV/AIDS.

Academic Subject: ADMINISTRATION OF JUSTICE

We View Juvenile Delinquents Differently Than Adult Criminals

by Robert Agnew

On the first day of my juvenile delinquency class I play a trick on my students. I pass out a description of a crime that has occurred: Someone walks into a bank, points a gun at a teller, and demands money. It is a toy gun, but the teller believes it is real and gives the bank robber several hundred dollars. The robber later spends most of the money on luxury items before being caught. I ask the students what the court should do to this robber. Unbeknownst to the students, the robber is described as a "7-year-old boy" in half the descriptions and a "32-year-old man" in the other half (the actual crime was committed by a 7-year-old boy).

After the students have considered the case for a few minutes, I ask for volunteers to tell me what they think should be done to the "bank robber." Some of the students describe what might be considered "mild" reactions on the part of the court: The robber should receive counseling, should be closely monitored for a period of time, should perform some community service, or the like. Other students describe what might be considered "tough" reactions on the part of the court; most commonly, they state that the robber should be locked up for several years. The students, of course, are confused by the responses of many of their classmates. Those with the 7-year-old robber wonder how some of their classmates could be so cold-hearted as to recommend years of imprisonment, while those with the 32-year-old robber think some of their classmates are far too "soft" on crime.

I eventually tell the students that they are working with two different case studies and that this age discrepancy is the major reason for their different reactions. I then try to justify the trick I have played by telling the students that their different reactions to the 7- and 32-year-old robbers illustrate a very important point about juvenile delinquency: We tend to view juvenile delinquents differently than adult criminals.

If a juvenile breaks the law, we generally view that person as *immature and in need of our guidance and help*. There is no precise definition of immaturity, but notions of immaturity usually include one or more of the following: The individuals did not know that what they were doing was wrong; they did not appreciate the harm that their actions might cause; they could not control themselves; or they were easily led astray by others. They therefore do not deserve serious punishment. Rather, they need our help. So when a 7-year-old robs a bank, many students state that the major response of the court should be to provide that person with counseling. But if an adult breaks the law, we generally view that person as someone who *is responsible for his or her behavior and deserves to be punished.* So most students have no qualms about sending a 32-year-old who robbed a bank to prison for many years.

Many students take exception when I characterize juveniles in this way. They state that many juvenile offenders know exactly what they are doing and that these offenders should be punished just as severely as adults. They often describe some horrifying crime committed in the recent past by a juvenile, and they state that this juvenile surely deserves the most serious punishment the law can provide.

I realize that many people feel this way. Certain juvenile offenders—especially older juveniles who commit serious crimes—are not viewed as all that different from adult offenders. And the justice system is starting to treat these offenders like adult criminals. So when I say that we view juvenile delinquents differently than adult criminals, an important exception should be noted. We often view older, serious juvenile offenders like adult offenders. I will talk more about this exception shortly. Aside from this important exception, we still tend to view juvenile delinquents differently than adult criminals. I provide my students with a few additional examples to illustrate this point.

There is the case of a 6-year-old girl in Florida who got into a fight with her 7-year-old friend. The 6-year-old girl repeatedly hit her 7-year-old friend with a piece of wood, while an older boy held the 7-year-old's arms behind her back. The 7-year-old's nose was damaged and her dress was soaked with blood by the time she arrived home to her mother. Her mother, of course, was outraged and immediately called the police. For legal reasons that I will not describe, there was some discussion of trying the 6-year-old girl as an adult. If tried as an adult, she would face a maximum penalty of fifteen years in prison and a $10,000 fine. This story made the national news, and people were outraged that such a young girl might be so severely penalized. They felt that the 6-year-old did not know what she was doing and that she needed guidance and help much more than punishment. Imagine the reaction, however, if a 30-year-old woman had committed this crime. People would be demanding the severest of penalties.

To give another example, a 6-year-old boy in California was charged with savagely beating a month-old baby. He was accused of kicking, punching, and beating the sleeping baby with a stick, possibly causing permanent brain damage. The 6-year-old was said to have done this to seek revenge against the family of the baby for allegedly harassing him. I asked the students in my class how the court should respond to this boy. This is a savage crime, but the young age of the boy led many in the class to talk of his immaturity and to argue that he is in desperate need of guidance and help. Again, imagine the difference in reaction if a 30-year-old man were charged with this crime.

With the exception of older juveniles who commit serious crimes, we clearly tend to view juvenile delinquents differently than adult criminals. We view juvenile delinquents as immature and in need of guidance and help, while we view adult criminals as fully responsible for their behavior and deserving of punishment. To illustrate, one recent national poll found that only 21 percent of the public said that rehabilitation should be the most important sentencing goal for *adults*, but 50 percent said that it should be the most important sentencing goal for *juveniles*.

Academic Subject: BIOLOGY

Bacteria: Enough to Give You an Ulcer

by Allan J. Tobin and Jennie Dusheck

In 1984, an obscure Australian physician named Barry Marshall secretly performed a dangerous experiment that would ultimately deprive some of the world's largest corporations of billions of dollars. Marshall's radical idea was born in 1979 when his colleague and friend J. Robin Warren noticed that tissues taken from ulcer patients were often infected with bacteria.

To find one bacterial infection in the stomach would have been strange; to find dozens was bizarre. The human stomach secretes acid so concentrated that few organisms survive it for more than a few minutes, let alone live and reproduce in it. Yet Warren found bacteria flourishing there.

Warren's discovery suggested an alternative to doctors' long-standing belief that ulcers are caused by excess stomach acid. Ulcers, every medical textbook reported, were caused by the oversecretion of stomach acid in people with overanxious, frustrated personalities. Such personality problems were thought to be aggravated by the stressful pace of modern life. But if a bacterium could infect the stomach, Marshall and Warren realized, maybe it could cause ulcers. Intrigued by this idea, Marshall began ordering biopsies for all his patients who had stomach problems. He found that nearly every patient with ulcers was infected with the same bacterium.

The most common kind of ulcer is a peptic ulcer, an open wound located where the stomach joins the small intestine, at the bottom of the stomach. The word peptic comes from the Greek word *peptein,* to digest. Nearly one in ten adults has a peptic ulcer. Some people with ulcers feel no discomfort, but most experience at least mild pain, and many suffer excruciating pain for weeks at a time throughout their adult lives. In rare cases, blood may pour from the wound so freely that the victim bleeds to death. The standard treatment for ulcers had always been a high-fat, bland diet, tranquilizers, psychotherapy, and, in severe cases, surgery. Mainly, however, doctors prescribed antacids—lots of antacids.

Antacids are the biggest-selling prescription drugs in the world. In 1992, Americans bought $4.4 billion worth of the drugs. Prescription antacids are remarkably effective at controlling the secretion of stomach acid, but remarkably ineffective at controlling ulcers. Ninety-five percent of ulcer patients have a new ulcer within 2 years of treatment. That means people who have ulcers take the $100-a-month antacids almost continuously. In a lifetime, an ulcer-sufferer can spend tens of thousands of dollars on antacids.

Yet, if ulcers were caused by a bacterium, a 2-week course of antibiotics might cure millions of people permanently of what would otherwise be a lifetime of suffering. If Marshall's hunch was right, he had very good news, although not for the companies selling antacids.

Marshall, however, had insignificant credentials as a doctor and none as a researcher. In 1980, he seemed to have no more chance of selling his idea to the biomedical community than his bacteria had of flourishing in the corrosive environment of the stomach. Nevertheless, in 1983, Marshall presented his hypothesis at a scientific conference in Brussels. His presentation was a disaster. He was unknown; he was young, inexperienced and overexcited; and he had a seemingly screwball idea. "He didn't have the demeanor of a scientist," recalled Martin Blaser, professor of medicine at Vanderbilt University. "He was strutting around the stage. I thought, this guy is nuts." When Marshall's presentation was over, his audience of eminent medical researchers shifted uneasily in their seats, embarrassed. A few laughed. They couldn't believe he was serious. Most bacteria can barely survive a brief passage through the stomach. How could they flourish there for months or years?

Besides, Marshall had no scientific evidence to back up his claim. Maybe, his audience told him, the bacteria had contaminated the stomach samples *after* the stomach tissues had been removed. Or maybe the bacteria was harmless and unrelated to the ulcers. Or maybe the bacteria were able to colonize the stomach as a *result* of the ulcer.

Marshall realized that the only way to settle these questions was to study the bacterium in an experimental animal. He needed to find an animal whose stomach could be infected with the bacterium. After returning to Australia, he began feeding the bacteria to rats. The bacteria died in the rats' stomachs without having any effect. He fed the bacteria to pigs, with the same result. Now he began to wonder, could the bacteria really infect a stomach? Maybe the researchers in Brussels had been right to laugh at him.

Desperate to prove that he was no nut, Marshall did something highly unusual (and controversial). First, he had a stomach exam and biopsy to make sure his stomach was healthy. Then he made an "ulcer bug" cocktail containing at least a billion bacteria, and, in a few swift gulps, drank it down. The cocktail was enough, he hoped, to infect his stomach. He told no one ahead of time—not the medical ethics board at the hospital, not his wife. They wouldn't have approved, he knew.

At first, nothing happened. Then, 9 days later, nausea woke him early and he vomited. For another week he was tired, irritable, and hoarse. He had headaches and foul breath. A second stomach exam and biopsy showed that his stomach was inflamed and swarming with bacteria.

By the third week, Marshall was lucky enough to have recovered completely. He had not proved that the bacteria could cause ulcers, or even that it could infect the stomach for years at a time. But he had done something that strongly suggested that the bacterium, still unnamed at the time, could at least infect a healthy human stomach—one that didn't already have an ulcer.

In time, other more-established researchers began to take an interest. Mainly they were interested in proving Marshall wrong. But by the end of the 1980s, evidence that the bacterium could infect the stomach was unassailable. In 1989, the bacterium was named *Helicobacter pylori* because of the bacterium's helical shape and because it was known to colonize the pylorus, near the stomach's exit. By 1993, definitive studies by other researchers had shown that some 80 percent of ulcers were caused by *H. pylori,* and were treatable with antibiotics.

Drug companies, initially somewhat negative about Marshall's idea, began to see a silver lining in the cloud the Australian had created. It was true that people treated with only $20 worth of antibiotics had a relapse rate of only about five to ten percent—which meant an ulcer sufferer would spend thousands of dollars less on drugs. On the other hand, infection by *H. pylori* turned out to be one of the most common bacterial infections in humans in the world—infecting up to half of all people worldwide. And mounting evidence suggested that chronic infection by *H. pylori* not only caused ulcers but also increased the risk of developing stomach cancer. Here was a market for antibiotics consisting of billions of people. Marshall's cloud definitely had a silver lining.

By 1993, drug companies were hastily developing new diagnostic tests for *H. pylori* and new antibiotics to treat the infection. Biotechnology companies were trying to develop a vaccine, to be given in childhood, that would protect against *H. pylori,* ulcers, and maybe even stomach cancer, a leading cause of death in Asia. In early 1994, experts at the National Institutes of Health declared antibiotics the official treatment for most ulcers. For the first time, doctors began treating their patients with antibiotics that would offer a permanent cure. Change came slowly. By 1996, only one-third of doctors were prescribing antibiotics for ulcer patients. The rest continued to prescribe antacids only.

Marshall ultimately won acceptance as a scientist, earning a position on the faculty at the University of Virginia Medical School. He succeeded in part because he possessed many of the attributes of a good scientist. He had curiosity, intelligence, vision, and the dogged determination to pursue an idea—even when his stubbornness made him appear foolish. Perhaps most important, Marshall displayed an unusual independence of thought that allowed him to pursue an idea unimaginable to more dogmatic thinkers.

Academic Subject: BUSINESS

The Boss Feels Your Pain

by Sharon Begley

At work, emotional intelligence makes a difference. One Airline CEO was a master of the personal touch, spending hours with baggage handlers and pilots, getting to know his employees and their jobs; he persuaded them to accept pay cuts in return for an ownership stake. The concessions put the company—Western Airlines—so solidly in the black that the CEO was able to sell it to Delta for $860 million. Another CEO berated underlings in front of other workers, cut one third of the work force and so embittered the survivors that his airline—Delta—lost its reputation for customer service and suffered an exodus of gifted managers. The exec admitted he had devastated the work force, and the board of directors, led by the first CEO, forced him out last year.

In any test of financial savvy, management principles or IQ, the two CEOs would have dueled to a draw. The difference was their ability to handle relationships, argues Daniel Goleman in his new book, *Working With Emotional Intelligence* (352 pages. Bantam. $25.95). Building on his 1995 blockbuster, *Emotional Intelligence,* which settled onto best-seller lists for 78 weeks, psychologist and former New York Times reporter Goleman now probes how EI [Emotional Intelligence]—the ability to master such "emotional competencies" as self-control, initiative, empathy, inspiration, political savvy and cooperation—relates to the world of work. As he did in his earlier book, Goleman masterfully explains the neuroscience of how a low EI thwarts people's full intellectual potential by, for instance, flooding the brain with stress hormones that impair memory, learning and thinking. The heart of the book, though, is an analysis of data collected from more than 150 firms on what distinguishes so-so performers from superstars. The results deal a body blow to anyone who worships at the shrine of IQ: conventional intelligence "takes second position to emotional intelligence in determining outstanding job performance," Goleman finds. In jobs ranging from copier repairman to scientist, IQ accounts for no more than 25 percent of the difference between, say, a successful high tech entrepreneur and a failed one. In another surprise, the contribution of IQ shrinks and the contribution of EI rises with the difficulty of a job and how high it ranks in an organization. Based on traits that companies say distinguish stars from also-rans, EI "carries much more weight than IQ" in determining success at the top, Goleman concludes.

Which is not to say that cognitive ability, knowledge and technical skill don't matter. You need some benchmark cognitive ability and knowledge to become, say, an electrical engineer or chief financial officer in the first place. It's a safe bet that one CFO with a business degree from a top school is about as smart, IQ-wise, as another. But school smarts get you only into the corner office. With everyone clustered in the same IQ range, the competitive edge comes from qualities that show more variation. And that's emotional intelligence. Of 59 high-tech entrepreneurs, Goleman relates in a typical example, those judged highest in EI skills like seeking feedback and setting goals had the highest sales and most employees.

EI does not mean being nice. And it does not mean touchy-feely management. It is, instead, the ability to manage your own emotions and handle relationships. For instance, empathy is a form of EI that gives a supersalesman at Nordstrom his ability to serve customers. EI is not set at birth, but can be learned.

For all its strengths, however, *Working With Emotional Intelligence* never quite transcends the business-book genre. Goleman devotes 200-plus pages to such worn ideas as "When to Be Tough" and "The Art of Networking," for instance. More disturbing, the many examples of CEOs and other people in top positions who have the emotional intelligence of a snake—but still were CEOs—undermine the case for EI's indispensability in business. (Goleman explained in an interview that people get promoted for lots of dumb reasons.) But even if you accept that EI determines who excels, you have to wonder if it should. Coleman describes how 112 entry-level accountants were judged more or less successful (by their bosses) according to their level of EI rather than their actual skills. No wonder so many auditors fail to notice cooked books.

Control freak: A low-EI boss may do your job, too, making you feel unsure and inept. *The loner:* Computer whizzes who flunk teamwork stagnate; the sociable ones star. *I'm OK:* Accountants with the most self-confidence, not the best skills, got top ratings.

Academic Subject: CHEMISTRY

The Chemical Foundation of Life

by Allan J. Tobin and Jennie Dusheck

Alchemy and Chemistry

In the spring of 1992, Texas A&M University Professor of Chemistry John Bockris received a friendly phone call from a man named Joe Champion. Champion said he was a Tennessee inventor who had developed a method for turning silver into gold. Gold is worth 20 times more than silver, so Champion's discovery, if legitimate, would be better than owning a gold mine. Besides offering to share the valuable secret with Bockris, Champion also offered $200,000 for Bockris to investigate and test the potentially lucrative new technique. It was an offer that Bockris couldn't resist, and he soon had the members of his laboratory testing Champion's technique.

Champion came to Texas to show Bockris and his assistants how to mix the right chemicals (which included one of the components of gun powder) to create gold. As long as Champion was helping out in the lab, the technique seemed to work. But when Champion left town, the technique mysteriously failed.

Bockris' colleagues at Texas A&M were acutely embarrassed. What Bockris was attempting was plain old-fashioned **alchemy**—an ancient pseudoscience one of whose aims was to turn "base" metals, such as lead or copper, into silver or gold. Alchemy reached the height of its popularity during the Middle Ages (about 700 years ago) and was completely discredited in the nineteenth century. Silver, gold, copper, and lead are all **elements**—substances that cannot be reduced to simpler substances by chemical means. In this chapter we will see why no element can be transformed into another element by chemical reactions.

What happened to Champion and Bockris? Champion spent a couple of years in jail, charged with criminal fraud in another case. A third man who provided the $200,000 to Bockris, was charged by the federal Securities and Exchange Commission with fraudulently selling unregistered stocks to innocent investors. Texas A&M froze Bockris' research account, refusing to give him any more of the probably ill-gotten $200,000. And 11 of Bockris' 39 colleagues in the chemistry department formally demanded that Bockris resign from the university, charging that he was ruining their reputations as chemists. Bockris kept his job, however, while still arguing that elements could be changed one into another by chemical means. Ultimately, he abandoned his research in alchemy and turned to more conventional studies of the chemical bond.

Academic Subject: HISTORY/COMMUNICATION

History of Communication

by Sue DeWine, Melissa K. Gibson, and Matthew J. Smith

Helping individuals communicate effectively has been the goal of communication scholars for hundreds of years. The human race established a system of communication that supported the development of society. Communication, as a field, began to emerge in ancient times and still serves as the foundation for much of what we believe about how human beings interact. Knowing something about these early writers will help you understand [communication principles]. We invite you to imagine another time and place when the field of communication was just beginning.

Ancient Greece

The field of communication traces its history back over 2,500 years to ancient Greece when the spoken word was the dominant form of communication. Oral presentations were the most efficient way of spreading information and presenting legal and political arguments.

Imagine yourself in the following setting.

You cross the busy central marketplace in Athens, to attend the Lyceum, a school founded by Aristotle. Aristotle is a well-known philosopher and author on classical **rhetoric**, or the study of persuasion. You are training for public life, where you will defend your arguments in public in the ancient form of democratic government. Individual citizens must defend themselves in court without benefit of lawyers, so in a sense, each citizen must be a practicing lawyer.

However, if you are a woman, it is not appropriate for you to speak in public, and you are not allowed to attend schools of higher learning. There is a slight possibility you studied with Aspasia, the only known ancient Greek teacher of philosophy and rhetoric who was a woman. Allusions to her by other writers "help to confirm that Aspasia was indeed a real person, a teacher of rhetoric who shared her knowledge and political skill with [others]" (Jarratt & Ong, 1995, p. 10). Some scholars feel we cannot overestimate how extraordinary such behavior was for a woman in fifth-century, B.C., although women in earlier and later periods of history played a more public role.

If you are attending one of these schools, you listen to the philosopher/teachers' lectures in the open arena and you discuss philosophy, logic, ethics, and rhetoric with your classmates. Nearby, other contemporaries are engaged in athletic events and practice for war games because war is a dominant preoccupation in these times.

Aristotle, in his famous book *The Rhetoric,* defined rhetoric as having five distinct parts:

- *Invention,* or finding all the available means of argument.
- *Arrangement,* or the way in which a speaker organizes the main points of the speech.
- *Style,* which is the use of language and phrasing.
- *Delivery,* or the presentation of the material and all the voice inflections and gestures.
- *Memory,* the ability to remember all the major points without the use of notes.

Attention to **audience analysis** began here. Insisting that the speaker adapt what is said to the particular audience being addressed is a critical canon of rhetoric. Storytelling, dramatic performances, and poetry readings by actors and orators became dominant forms of entertainment. These individuals were honored and respected (see Cooper, 1932).

In ancient Greece the status of a speaker was just as important as what was said. The Greeks often confused authority with being right: because you were in a position of authority, you were right. Conley (1990) suggested that "public discussion, where options were debated and consensus sought, was evidently the traditional way in which decisions were reached" (1990, p. 2). However, it was not only the argument that counted. "The status of the speaker who presented the argument is all important" (p. 2). So, while we like to refer to ancient Greece as the birthplace of democracy, all men and women were certainly not equal.

There were those who argued for more equality. Plato, for example, implemented two basic principles that placed rhetoric, or the art of persuasion, at the forefront of Greek public life. He argued that (1) power should reside in the people as a whole and (2) high offices should go to those who are selected by the citizens as the best individuals for the job. These were revolutionary ideas that ultimately placed persuasive speech at the center of the new democracy.

> In civil disputes, persuasion established claims where no clear truth was available. Persuasive speech, too, could depose or empower tyrants, determine public policy, and administer laws. The public speaker was inseparable from the business of government and civic affairs, and early on some enterprising orators turned to teaching the art of persuasive speech as well as practicing it. (Bizzell & Herzberg, 1990, p. 2)

These "enterprising orators" were called **Sophists.** They were itinerant, or part-time traveling teachers. When a democratic form of government was implemented in 450 B.C. they were in great demand. The typical political structure built around clans and families was replaced with a system of representative government, which cut across all former barriers of influence. These teachers traveled from one town to the next teaching the skill of argument. They were severely criticized for not seeking the truth and instead practicing what some saw as the tricks of persuading others. However, the Sophists saw themselves as problem solvers.

References

Bizzell, P., & Herzberg, B. (1990). *The Rhetorical Tradition: Readings from Classical Times to the Present.* Boston, MA: St. Martin's Press.

Conley, T. M. (1990). *Rhetoric in the European Tradition.* Chicago, IL: University of Chicago Press.

Cooper, L. (1932). *The Rhetoric of Aristotle.* New York: Appleton-Century-Crofts.

Jarratt, S., & Ong, R. (1995). " Aspasia: Rhetoric, Gender, and Colonial Ideology." In A. A. Lunsford (Ed.), *Reclaiming Rhetorica: Women in the Rhetorical Tradition* (pp. 9–24). Pittsburgh, PA: University of Pittsburgh.

Excerpted and adapted from: Sue DeWine, Melissa K. Gibson, and Matthew J. Smith, *Exploring Human Communication,* pp. 16–17.

Academic Subject: COMMUNICATION

Communicating Nonverbally

by Sue DeWine, Melissa K. Gibson, and Matthew J. Smith

In my many years of participating in various athletic events, I have witnessed many examples of communication, both verbal and nonverbal. The best example of communication and its importance is in baseball. Baseball involves a great deal of communication without spoken words.

In baseball, the majority of the coaching is done through motions and nonverbal messages. For example, the act of touching the bill of a baseball hat may be a signal from coach to player to steal a base. These actions vary in order to relay different messages. It is these signals that enable the coaches to communicate with one another and the players on the field.

Another example of this unspoken tongue is when the coach or manager goes to the pitcher's mound and touches his right arm and points toward the bullpen. This signal indicates that the bullpen coach is to send in the right-handed pitcher. These unspoken signs are a very effective form of communication, even though the conventional thought is that communication involves words.

—Ramon, third-year college student

As Ramon explains, our communication is not limited to words only. Just as coaches and players in a baseball game rely on hand gestures and signals to communicate information across a playing field, we too rely on nonverbal messages to create common connections with others. **Nonverbal communication** refers to all nonword messages that we transmit from person to person. In many ways, nonverbal communication is the most powerful form of communication that we, as human beings, have at our disposal.

The old cliché, "A picture is worth a thousand words" illustrates this point. Remember back to the women's gymnastics competition of the 1996 Olympic Games. As the last gymnast on the United States team left to compete, Kerri Strug needed to complete the vault to give her team the gold medal. The world watched as on her first attempt she severely injured her leg on a maneuver. With one more run to go, the world waited breathlessly as she hopped in agony to the end of the mat, completed the run despite being in excruciating pain, and earned her team the gold. Did Kerri Strug need to explain to you the pain, shock, and pressure she was feeling? No, it was evident in her posture and facial expressions. And even though she later talked about what she experienced with reporters, we needed only to look at her grimaced face and see her tear-filled eyes to understand her pain. Sometimes words just can't communicate enough of what we're really feeling.

When you use nonverbal methods to send messages, you are using the most basic—and often the most believed—form of communication available. Imagine that your friend asks you how you're coping with the loss of your grandparent. Although you reply "Just fine," a tear silently trickles down your face. This nonverbal message—a tear—says something very different. However, even though they may have more impact than verbal messages, nonverbal messages may also be the most ambiguous. Can a tear communicate more than just sadness? Of course, tears are used to communicate a variety of feelings in human beings, from sadness to frustration to outright happiness.

[Here], we'll look more closely at this powerful but implicit form of communication that involves more than just words.

- First, we'll begin by discussing the similarities and differences between verbal and nonverbal messages.
- Then, we'll see how nonverbal messages function in our everyday communication.
- We'll study different types of nonverbal messages including how distance and space, body movement, touch, objects, and clothing have the potential to send very important messages. Even silence is indeed golden in its power to communicate.

Verbal vs. Nonverbal Messages

Similarities Between Verbal and Nonverbal Messages

How is nonverbal communication similar to verbal communication? First, both forms of communication are generally considered symbolic although not all communication researchers agree upon this entirely. If you say that you have a small tan dog named Abby, you're using symbols to stand for a pet you own. The words you use to describe your pet—small, tan, and dog—have agreed-upon symbolic meanings that paint a picture in your mind of what Abby is and looks like. J. K.

Burgoon and T. J. Saine (1978) explain that nonverbal messages become symbolic when they represent an abstraction. When you see someone smiling (nonverbal act) and attach meaning that the person is happy, a symbolic link has been created because the nonverbal act has served to represent the abstract thought "happiness."

Another similarity between verbal and nonverbal messages is that they are both individually produced. The messages that we send are, in a sense, personal and subjective. The rhythmic tapping of your feet when you're excited is individually produced. In another person, this same tapping may be a nonverbal gesture done to indicate boredom or frustration. Interestingly, research on twins and triplets shows that they often develop a language of their own: The verbal messages that they devise are subjective and personal to them and their siblings.

Finally, both verbal and nonverbal messages are subject to interpretation. In both message forms, what you say and what you do must be interpreted by others. The people we interact with attach meaning to our verbal and nonverbal messages and alter their behavior accordingly. If a woman tells her fiancé that she has called off the wedding (verbal message) and he begins to cry (nonverbal message), they are both interpreting messages and acting accordingly. In these ways, it is possible to see the characteristics that verbal and nonverbal messages share. Both are symbolic, individually produced, and subject to interpretation.

How Nonverbal Messages Differ From Verbal Messages

Although nonverbal communication is similar to verbal communication in certain respects, it is also quite different in important ways (see Figure 3.1).

Nonverbal communication is:

- More primitive.
- More uncontrollable.
- More believable.
- Continuous.
- Unstructured.
- More widely understood.

Nonverbal communication is a more primitive form of message-sending than is verbal communication (Hickson & Stacks, 1985). Some researchers believe that nonverbal communication is innate, that we are born with certain nonverbal understandings. For example, usually it takes a baby a year or longer to learn simple utterances like "Da Da" or "Ma Ma." To learn verbal communication, a child needs advanced muscle development and socialization. This is not the case with nonverbal communication. From the moment babies are born, they begin to communi-

Figure 3.1 Similarities and Differences in Nonverbal Communications

Characteristic	*Verbal Message*	*Nonverbal Message*
Symbolic	X	X
Individually produced	X	X
Subject to interpretation	X	X
More primitive		X
More uncontrollable		X
More believable		X
Continuous		X
Unstructured		X
Widely understood		X

cate nonverbally through smiles, cries, yawns, and shrieks. Is the ability to smile when happy or frown when sad learned through imitation of parents and other adults, or is it an innate ability? Does anyone ever tell a child how to smile or how to frown? Not really, so perhaps nonverbal communication is an innate form of communication.

To further back up the claim that nonverbal communication is innate is the fact that biological forces govern many of our nonverbal actions. In many—but obviously not all—instances, our nonverbal messages are often more uncontrollable than our verbal communications (Hickson & Stacks, 1985). If a rude stranger cuts in front of you in the checkout line at the grocery, what can you do? When faced with a situation like this, you have several options. You could politely ask her to move or you could swear at her loudly. Generally, you have more control over these verbal actions than over the nonverbal messages you might be sending. Even if you remained silent, your clenched hands and blushing face indicate that you are really angry with that stranger. Although you may have chosen to do nothing to communicate your anger to this person, many of your nonverbal actions—like shaking, blinking, blushing, and trembling—can communicate loudly despite your intentions.

Nonverbal messages have considerable impact and can be more believable than verbal messages. When verbal and nonverbal messages contradict each other, you are more likely to believe the nonverbal message. Psychologists and counselors must practice this every day in their jobs. When individuals seek a professional to hear their problems and concerns, they are expecting the psychologist or counselor to be an attentive listener. If the counselor is avoiding eye contact, drawing pictures in a notebook, and turning away from the patient, the patient may believe the nonverbal message ("I'm not interested in what you're saying") over the verbal promise that the counselor made ("I'm here to listen to your concerns").

Another characteristic of nonverbal communication is that it is a relatively continuous process, whereas verbal communication is more discontinuous. Verbal communication is composed of disconnected units broken down into words, phrases, and sentences. Each word and sentence has a distinct beginning and end. Unfortunately, it is not quite as easy to turn off nonverbal messages. We cannot turn off nonverbal messages being sent, such as when we wear certain clothing or have body odor. Someone who is speaking loudly in the library can quit speaking instantaneously, but someone with foul body odor on a hot humid day in a crowded subway car will continue to send that message until he or she leaves your physical presence.

Another interesting characteristic of nonverbal communication is its unstructured nature as compared to that of verbal communication. Language follows a specific linguistic structure, such as rules of grammar. As children, we must be taught that in English a verb follows a noun. It takes us a while to understand this and you can often hear young children confusing the sentence structure saying, "Go I to the store." The structured nature of language is readily apparent if you try to learn a new language. For example, when English speakers learn Spanish, they may be confused by the grammatical rule that adjectives follow the word they describe. In English, the adjective *red* would precede the noun *book* to say "the red book." However in Spanish, the adjective *rojo* would usually follow the noun *el libro* to say "el libro rojo." On the other hand, nonverbal communication tends to be more unstructured. There really is no book of grammar for nonverbal communication. For example, waving to someone does not follow the same structure or rules of grammar as a verbal message does. Waving your hand could mean that you are saying hello, or that you are saying goodbye, or maybe even that you are flagging someone down for help. In this sense, we can't assume that waving your hand has a predictable pattern of meaning for a community of people.

Lastly, nonverbal messages are often more widely understood than verbal messages. Sometimes, nonverbal messages help us understand one another when other forms of communication fail. In particular, when we do not speak the same language, nonverbal methods may be the only hope for communication. Two communicators with different language backgrounds can still communicate through nonverbal gestures, expressions, and messages. Like a game of charades, it is possible to communicate your thoughts and feelings without uttering a word. Sometimes verbal messages are just not understood. For example, in the following story a student discovered that nonverbal messages helped her communicate when verbal messages were ineffective.

> This past summer I lived in Virginia and taught a special-education summer school session for autistic, severely retarded, preschool crack babies, and emotionally disturbed children. Due to the fact that the majority of my students could not communicate verbally, I had to find other ways to communicate effectively with them. I quickly learned that eye contact was important. The students needed direct attention and contact in order for them to understand that I was talking to them.
>
> I also learned other physical cues to help students understand my requests. I learned to get through language barriers effectively. I realized how important it is to have different approaches to explaining something in order for different audiences to understand your point.
>
> —Alyson, second-year college student

As Alyson discovered, she was able to communicate a mountain of information to her vocally- and psychologically-challenged students using nonverbal means (Heimlich & Mark, 1990). In this case, nonverbal messages were able to reach an audience that could not comprehend and decode language.

References

Burgoon, J. K., & Saine, T. J. (1978). *The Unspoken Dialogue: An Introduction to Nonverbal Communication.* Boston, MA: Houghton-Mifflin.

Heimlich, E. P., & Mark, A. J. (1990). *Paraverbal Communication with Children: Not Through Words Alone. New York: Plenum Press.*

Hickson, M. L. III., & Stacks, D. W. (1985).*Nonverbal Communication: Studies and Applications.* Dubuque, IA: Wm. C. Brown Publishers.

Academic Subject: INTERCULTURAL COMMUNICATION

Improving Intercultural Communication

by Sue DeWine, Melissa K. Gibson, and Matthew J. Smith

Recognizing Ethnocentrism

As the world shrinks more and more, our opportunities to practice communicating with other cultures increase dramatically. Today, it would not be out of the ordinary for a teenager in Brazil and a teenager in Australia to be Internet conversation partners, nor would it be unusual to be sitting in a multicultural classroom in kindergarten, high school, or college. So, learning to communicate across cultures is perhaps more important than at any time in the past. Generations before ours found intercultural communication to be a novelty; younger generations find it a necessity.

Perhaps the first step toward improving intercultural communication is to be aware of ethnocentric tendencies. **Ethnocentrism** is the tendency to view one's own culture as superior to others. It is important to understand that ethnocentrism is neither wholly avoidable nor wholly undesirable. Most of us can't help but look at our own culture positively. And, to some degree, it is important to be proud of your culture, to carry on the values, beliefs, and practices that comprise your heritage. Ethnocentrism becomes a barrier to effective communication when it prevents you from viewing *other* cultures positively or respecting other cultural practices and beliefs. Being able to mentally say, "I understand that I may be shocked by the practice of eating dogs in Malaysia because it is not practiced in my own culture, but it does not make the practice right or wrong" is the first step toward improving intercultural communication.

By recognizing your own ethnocentrism, you can begin to appreciate the diversity of cultural affiliations around you. Respecting people different from you can be difficult, particularly given the environmental, parental, and societal influences that surround you. Being curious about other people and being mindful that differences do exist are important steps to improving your intercultural understanding.

Rather than resisting intercultural differences, we, as a society, need to embrace intercultural differences. Perhaps the group No Doubt says it best in their song, "Different People," when they remark, "But the most amazing thing/That I've seen in my time/Are all the different people/And all their different minds."

Avoiding Stereotypes

The second step toward improving intercultural communication is to avoid stereotypes. **Stereotyping,** or the practice of holding rigid conceptions or categories about a group of people, may be a detriment to intercultural communication. Stereotyping is a necessary evil. If we didn't stereotype initial information, we would be too overwhelmed to function on a daily basis. What if every person you passed on the street had to be mentally categorized as either a "male" or a "female" through a formal process of deductive thinking. Walking down the street would soon become a nightmare! Instead, we tend to "stereotype" gender according to physical characteristics, such as facial features, physical attributes (i.e., breasts), and vocal patterns. Sometimes, however, after further investigation, our initial stereotypes are proven wrong.

Stereotyping is an attempt to lump all people of a certain culture or group together under a common set of characteristics. While we tend to think of stereotyping as a negative practice, it can actually be positive in nature. Think about the following statements. Asians are intelligent. African Americans are superior athletes. Even positive attributions could be problematic to intercultural communication. Simply applying these statements to the "all" test proves the point. Are *all* Asians intelligent? Are *all* African Americans superior athletes? The answer is obviously no. Whenever you hear yourself saying, "All men act like . . ." or "All Muslims are . . .," be wary about what you are about to communicate.

Ultimately, it is important to realize that as the world shrinks, so too should the perception that isolation is neither possible nor desirable in our contemporary society. With increases in technology, transportation, and economic opportunities, improving intercultural communication skills is not something that you *should* do, but something that you *must* do in order to be a productive citizen of an increasingly complex world. Avoiding ethnocentric tendencies and stereotyping seems like a simple two-step recipe for improving your skills, but rarely is intercultural communication that easy. Communicating across cultures is difficult, challenging, and certainly worthwhile.

Excerpted from: Sue DeWine, Melissa K. Gibson, and Matthew J. Smith, *Exploring Human Communication*, pp. 188–190.

Academic Subject: PSYCHOLOGY/SOCIOLOGY

Raising Daughters and Sons: Different Challenges

by Karen Benjamin, Ph.D., and Lynn Hawley, M.A.

Role Models for Girls

A lot has been said lately about the importance of good role models for children and particularly for young women. Historically, a young girl would look to her own mother and other female family members for guidance and training in the domestic arts. The roles of mother and wife were paramount and were the only aspirations "decent" girls were supposed to have in life. M. Carey Thomas, the first president of Bryn Mawr College, wrote in her diary in the 1870s that she desperately wanted to pursue higher education but could not convince her parents. No one in her family knew of any women who had attended college, and Thomas said when she finally met a woman who had attended Vassar, she was impressed. Women who wanted to experience a life other than a purely domestic one were in for some serious challenges, one of which was a lack of role models.

Two major events in the twentieth century would change this situation for girls. The first was the civil-rights movement of the 1950s and 1960s. In this politically charged atmosphere, women risked their lives. Young women saw on television other women being arrested and beaten. They saw women asserting their rights and speaking before crowds. They saw women organizing marches and sit-ins. Women like Ella Baker, Rosa Parks, JoAnn Gibson Robinson and Ann Moody demonstrated to American women of all races that women were capable of political action, and they inspired an entire generation of women to want more in their lives. They expanded horizons of young women everywhere through their activities for the movement.

Second, starting in the 1960s, modern feminists argued that gender stereotyping starts very young and that young girls were being inundated with messages from family, school, church and society in general about appearance and acceptable roles for women. Feminists argued that it was no wonder that little girls could only imagine themselves as mommies and housewives—one had only to look at television and advertisements from this period to see the limited portrayal of women as primarily domestic. Little girls of a generation ago were getting the message loudly and clearly—you will be a housewife and mother.

Feminists, however, felt role models for girls were an important part of the process to expand the choices available to women. How can you imagine yourself as a doctor or a scientist if you never see women in the media in these roles? The first phase of this process took place in school textbooks back in the 1970s, making sure that there were equal representations of men and women in a variety of professions. The feminist leaders also pushed for activities such as "Take Your Daughter to Work Day," where young girls could see women in the workplace and discover any number of career paths they might wish to pursue. Organizations such as NOW also pushed the media to put more women's sports on air so that little girls could see women working as professional athletes. In these ways and many others, the modern feminist movement wanted girls to have choices.

Now, young girls are raised with far different aspirations than their grandmothers ever had. We are now experiencing the result of expanding the choice of role models for girls. Students in women's history classes have a difficult time grasping a time when women were so limited because so many of them have mothers who work outside of the home; they have fathers who want them to pursue higher education, and they have friends who expect them to have a career. They have role models in the media and in their personal lives who inspire them to dream big dreams for themselves. Role models for girls have proven to be an important part of the liberation of women from an exclusively domestic role.

Building a Healthier Boy

Since 1982—after the landmark publication of Carol Gilligan's book *In a Different Voice: Psychological Theory and Women's Development*—much attention has been given to the ways in which girls develop. Gilligan's book, which inspired Take Our Daughters to Work Day, made it clear that psychological development is a two-dimensional scene. However, while girls' horizons have expanded, boys' [horizons] have narrowed. In the wake of the feminist movement, normal boy behavior—such as an abundance of energy and an urge to conquer—has come to be considered pathological.

New studies, however, are finding new meanings in the things boys have done for ages. In fact, one of the hottest new fields of inquiry in psychological research is the study of boys. In the past two years, several noteworthy books on boys' development have been released such as *Real Boys: Rescuing Our Sons From the Myths of*

Boyhood, Raising Cain: Protecting the Emotional Life of Boys, and *The Wonder Boys.* Additionally, Carol Gilligan, who chairs the gender studies department at Harvard, is now supervising work on males as well.

So what exactly are researchers discovering about boys? First, it seems that even as infants, boys and girls behave differently. A recent study at Children's Hospital in Boston found that boy babies are more emotionally expressive; girls are more reflective (that means boy babies tend to cry when they're unhappy; girl babies suck their thumbs). This could indicate that girls are innately more able to control their emotions. Additionally, boys have higher levels of testosterone and lower levels of the neurotransmitter seratonin, which inhibits aggression and impulsivity. That may explain why more males than females carry through with suicide, become alcoholics, and are diagnosed with ADD.

One of the biggest discoveries is that boys encounter their first crisis point—stages in social and emotional development where things can go very wrong—earlier than girls. According to Gilligan, there is an outbreak of symptoms in boys at 5, 6 and 7 just like are seen in girls at 11, 12 and 13. Problems at this young age can include bed-wetting and separation anxiety. According to William Pollack, head of the Center for Men at Boston's McLean Hospital and author of *Real Boys,* boys at this age begin to repress normal feelings like love because of social pressure. Pollack says that the pressure boys place on one another to adhere to what he calls the "Boy Code" is enormous and that boys shut down their emotions to avoid ridicule and ostracization from peers. He believes that the "Boy Code" manifests from the rigid beliefs society has about acceptable behavior for boys. Pollack says that because of the "Boy Code," boys have only one acceptable outlet: anger. Dan Kindlon, an assistant professor of psychiatry at Harvard Medical School and co-author of *Raising Cain,* agrees. He states, "the feminist movement has done a great job at convincing people that women can be nurturing and a mother and a tough trial lawyer at the same time, but we haven't done that as much with men. We are afraid that if they are too soft, that is all they can be."

A second crisis point for boys occurs around the same time that girls start stumbling, in early adolescence. By then, boys go one step further in their drive to be "real guys." According to Dan Kindlon and co-author Michael Thompson, they partake in a "culture of cruelty," enforcing male stereotypes on one another. "Anything tender, anything compassionate or too artistic is labeled gay. The homophobia of boys in the 11, 12 and 13 range is stronger than the force of gravity," says Thompson. Boys who refuse to fit the mold suffer.

So what is a parent to do? Psychological research shows that a strong parental bond is the most important protection against everything from smoking to suicide.

Contrary to popular belief, boys need just as much love and attention as girls, although they often do not know how to ask for it. Essentially, to save our sons from the emotional scarring which comes from trying to adhere to the "Boy Code," we need to keep connected to them. Don't be surprised, though, if your son pushes away your displays of affection and resists your attempts at giving him attention. Ironically, the very love and attention your son needs to help him cope with the "Boy Code" is prohibited by the Boy Code itself. So what should you do if your son protests your attempts at giving him love and attention? Keep at it. Your attempts may not seem to be doing anything but, in the end, they will.

Characteristics of a Good Father

- Provides time and space for his children to grow.
- Acts as a role model.
- Balances nurturing and discipline with play and adventure.
- Acts as a bridge to the outside world.
- Encourages his children to explore and take risks.
- Looks beyond his own comfort to meet the needs of his children.
- Is sensitive and flexible.
- Accepts responsibility for helping his children realize their potential.

Excerpted from: Karen Benjamin, "Raising Sons: Building a Healthier Boy" and Lynn Hawley, "Role Models for Girls." *Parenting Exchange*, March 2002, Vol. 5, No.3, pp. 1–2, 4–5. Reprinted by permission.

Academic Subject: SOCIOLOGY/CULTURE

I Want My Son to Be Proud

by Casey Kasem

When he was 12, my son, Mike, walked into our living room and said to me, "Dad, I hate Arabs."

I was shocked. My parents' background is Lebanese. I thought I'd taught Mike to be proud of his Arab heritage. Of course, like most kids born here, he thought of himself as American, period.

I asked why he hated Arabs. Mike said it was because of what he saw in films and on TV.

As a student at Detroit's Wayne State University, I'd learned how media stereotypes can create public attitudes. But that lesson only hit me emotionally when I saw how it had affected my son's self-image. I became more aware of how traditional Arab stereotypes get full play: from Rudolph Valentino's 1921 portrayal of *The Sheik* (with its memorable line, "When an Arab sees a woman he wants, he takes her"); to bad Arabs with big swords pursuing everyone across the desert, from The Three Stooges and Hope & Crosby to Beatty & Hoffman; all the way to recent films, where Arabs appear only as terrorists. At the same time, the positive contributions of Arabs throughout history—and of the Arab-American community—are skipped over as if they didn't exist.

That imbalance creates racism.

Americans with Arab heritage who have contributed to our nation include innovators in science and medicine like Dr. Michael DeBakey, the pioneer heart surgeon, and Professor Elias Corey, winner of the 1990 Nobel Prize for chemistry; entertainers like Paula Abdul and Paul Anka; political figures like John Sununu, President Bush's former chief of staff; George Mitchell, former Senate Majority Leader; and Donna Shalala, President Clinton's Secretary of Health and Human Services; and sports figures like Doug Flutie, the 1984 Heisman trophy-winner who is now a quarterback for the Calgary Stampeders, and Tony Seikaly, the pro baseball star.

Recently, I asked prominent Americans of Arab descent how they had dealt with racism. The answers ranged from confronting it head-on to staying silent. But, in every case, they rose above it.

James Abourezk, a former Senator who heads the American Arab Anti-Discrimination Committee (ADC), confronted the racism. Abourezk, whose parents were Lebanese, was called a "damn Jew" by some people in his hometown of Wood, SD, who knew nothing about Arabs or Lebanese.

Arab-bashing ballooned in the 70s. After the Abscam scandal, where FBI agents posed as oil sheiks to "sting" law-breaking members of Congress, outraged Arab-Americans asked for Abourezk's help. Turning down another term as Senator, he founded the ADC in 1980. The organization, which calls attention to instances of bias, today has 30,000 members in more than 70 cities. Abourezk, who was once nicknamed the "Syrian Sioux," also defends the rights of Native Americans.

"You look at popular media," he says, "and you don't find any Arab or Arab-American portrayed in a positive light. The last one was Danny Thomas in the TV shows [in the 50s and 60s], and then they were called Lebanese. I think the only movie where I've seen a positive Arab was in Kevin Costner's *Robin Hood*. But 99.5 percent of all portrayals of Arabs are vicious. *That's* why Arab-Americans are invisible.

"We've found in ADC that some Arab-Americans have changed their names to make them sound more Anglo, because they just don't want to get in trouble," he adds. For example, F. Murray Abraham—the American-born, Oscar-winning actor (*Amadeus*)—uses an initial because, as he told one reporter, his Syrian name, Fahrid, "would typecast me as a sour Arab out to kill everyone."

Joseph Jacobs grew up in Brooklyn, where the goal was to blend in as Americans. He worried less about taunts like "camel jockey" and more about whether his mother spoke Arabic in front of his friends. Today, he feels lucky to have his heritage: "The ethics, the pride, and sense of honor I learned in my ethnic community were important contributors to my business career."

Businessmen and intellectuals were Jacobs' role models. He recalls that many uneducated immigrants like his dad made great successes of themselves: "'What business are you in?' was a question I invariably heard asked when a Lebanese came to visit us."

Jacobs became a professor of chemical engineering, but his mother insisted he'd never be a success until he went into business for himself. So, in 1947, he started a one-man consulting firm. Today, Jacobs Engineering Group, based in Pasadena, is one of America's largest professional service firms—a billion-dollar international corporation.

Any racism he experienced as a youth, Jacobs says, gave him "additional incentive to *accomplish* something and get the respect of your peers." "Being accepted and respected in the American culture was a powerful motivator for me."

Candice Lightner's Lebanese-American mother was taught to "mainstream" and wouldn't teach her daughter to speak Arabic. But there was still Arabic culture at home. Lightner first experienced the pain of discrimination at 13, when a school friend's parents refused to let her visit Lightner because she was Lebanese. "I remember telling my parents and being very hurt," she says.

In 1980, after losing her daughter in a car accident caused by a drunk driver, Lightner founded MADD (Mothers Against Drunk Driving), lobbying across the nation for tougher laws. Today—2000 new laws later—"drunk driving is no longer socially acceptable," she says.

"The press would never *print* that I was an Arab-American," she asserts. "So, when I started doing live media, I'd bring it up." When Lightner protested the 1982 Israeli invasion of Lebanon, her boyfriend called her "anti-Semitic." Their relationship ended. Her non-Arab father knew better. "Honey, you *are* a Semite," he said. "That's the way I was raised," says Lightner. "We [Arabs and Jews] are all Semites."

Prejudice may have held back Fawaz "Tony" Ismail's dream of a pro football career. As a high school student in Texas, the Palestinian-American got good grades and excelled in soccer, track and weight-lifting. But, for three seasons, a new coaching staff didn't start him in a football game. "I felt I was being discriminated against because my name was different," he says.

In 1985, Ismail joined his father, selling flags on the road. Today, his Virginia-based Alamo Flag Co. is the largest retailer of flags and flag-related items in the United States. Ismail has sold Swedish flags in Minnesota, Italian and Irish flags in New York, and flags to citizens whose ancestries reach around the globe. [In September of 1993], he supplied the Palestinian flags and lapel pins for the historic signing of the Israeli-Palestinian peace accord at the White House.

Kathy Najimy grew up in San Diego proud of *her* heritage. The actress says she thought being Lebanese "was the coolest thing to be."

One of her feminist role models was Marlo Thomas, Danny's daughter and star of *That Girl* on TV (1966–1971). "She was the first actress in [television] history whose character was single, *independent,* had a job and didn't live with her parents!" says Najimy.

As an aspiring actress who wasn't built like a "Barbie doll," Najimy succeeded through comedy. She wrote and co-starred in a feminist cabaret hit, *The Kathy & Mo Show.* She played a bubbly nun in the popular film *Sister Act* and its sequel.

While she didn't suffer racism as a child, Najimy ran into bigotry in the late 1970s, when anti-Iranian sentiment swept the country. Technically, Iranians aren't Arabs, but it made no difference. Angered by the intellectual stupidity expressed in anti-Iranian bumper stickers, Najimy went around ripping them off cars.

People "need to have . . . someone they can feel *better* than—or hate," Najimy says. It's "sad," she adds, "because it comes from wanting to belong, to feel like part of a group."

The actress believes that all ethnic groups benefit from knowing their own heritage: "Identifying yourself as something strong and positive helps you to overcome the things that you're going to meet along the way as a woman."

Farouk El-Baz identified himself as a conservative Muslim raised in Cairo when he came to the United States in 1960 to earn a Ph.D. in geology. He soon learned that the beliefs of Egyptians about Americans were as incorrect as those of Americans about Arabs. "Americans did not really know about the Arab world—except for what was presented in the media, especially the movies," he recalls.

His accent was no hindrance when he joined America's space program in 1967. "In social settings, it even served as an icebreaker," he says. El-Baz worked on Apollo missions 8 through 17, helping to select landing sites, training astronauts in visual observations and photography, and naming features on the moon. He pioneered the use of space photography to locate groundwater and petroleum in the Earth's deserts. Today he directs Boston University's Center for Remote Sensing.

In 1971, El-Baz was interviewed for a TV special. Rick Berman, the sound man, was so impressed that in 1989, as executive producer of TV's *Star Trek: The Next Generation,* he named a shuttle craft El-Baz in the scientist's honor.

Arab-Americans are more visible today than when he was starting out, El-Baz says, but they still experience racism. "Racism originates from fear of the unknown or lack of knowledge," he says, adding that this is "usually alleviated by the spread of information on the Arab culture and its diversity."

Information is Helen Thomas' life. She fell in love with journalism in high school and has pursued it ever since.

A 50-year veteran with UPI, Thomas has covered eight Presidents and was the first woman admitted to Washington's Gridiron Club for journalists (1975)—as well as its first woman president (1992). She alternates with the AP reporter in opening Presidential news conferences and closes them with the words, "Thank you, Mr. President."

Thomas, whose parents were Lebanese, was raised in an ethnically mixed neighborhood in Detroit and doesn't recall feeling set apart from others. Her parents were determined to be American, says Thomas. They taught her "a sense of justice, love of freedom, democracy . . . really cherishing and appreciating what this country had given them and their children."

Thomas rejects labels and hyphens. "I think everybody who was born here or becomes a naturalized citizen is an American, period," she says. "You shouldn't have to have a hyphen between your nationality and your ethnic background or your religion or anything else." To improve race relations today, Thomas says she would teach tolerance in the schools, from kindergarten on.

In the years since my son said he hated Arabs, I've confronted Arab defamation in our society by highlighting positive contributions made by Arab-Americans. "Ask not what your country can do for you; ask what you can do for your country." Those sentiments, spoken by President Kennedy, were expressed earlier by, among others, an Arab-American philosopher and poet—Kahlil Gibran, author of *The Prophet*. He was proud of his Arab heritage and a champion of U.S. citizenship. Arab-Americans have reflected that sentiment ever since they first arrived, more than 100 years ago.

Academic Subject: SOCIOLOGY

In Defense of the Real American Family

by Kenneth D. Valdez

The shape of the American family has undergone a dramatic change over the last several decades. The once dominant "traditional nuclear family" is now accompanied by a variety of other familial forms. Many studies claim to demonstrate the adverse effects of these situations on children and on society. However, other studies take the position that these groups are just new and viable variations on the idea of what constitutes a family. There is mounting evidence that if researchers control for a wide spectrum of influences, they will arrive at a more accurate and positive assessment of the situation. If many variables are taken into consideration, the non-traditional family structure can be shown to have a potential for success comparable to that of the two-parent family.

Advocates of the "traditional" family as the only acceptable model base their claims on the interconnectedness of the structure of the family and its probability of success. In order to arrive at a realistic assessment of the merits and pitfalls of the various family groups, one must separate family interactions from family composition. Too often love and support are promoted as inherent qualities of the family that has both a mother and a father. This is a simplistic notion that does not acknowledge the reality of the dysfunctional two-parent family. As Alesia Montgomery and Robert Rossi, from the American Institute for Research, point out, in their 1994 report to the U.S. Department of Education, "two-parent households are not always stable and supportive and single-parent households are not always isolated and overwhelmed" (par. 4). They cite many factors other than family structure which might influence a child's probability of success in life including strong family cohesiveness, positive parental guidance, and supportive community networks. Some negative factors which are separate from the composition of the family and which could lead to problems are lack of parental warmth, neglect, and high levels of conflict within the family (par. 5).

Many studies substantiate the conclusion that family climate has the most direct effect on child development. Although single parent and blended families are presented with a unique set of challenges, stress occurs in all family groupings. Harmful home environments contribute to a variety of problems. Alesia Montgomery and Robert Rossi cite a study that correlates the risk of substance abuse with unstable home environments and the parents' permissive views on alcohol use (par. 13). Physical or sexual abuse have been shown to contribute to depression and antisocial behavior in children. Severe abuse or neglect often results in self-destructive behavior (par. 6). These are extreme examples of damaging influences, but many less obvious factors instigate behavioral problems.

Often studies which examine children's behavior focus on school readiness and success. In the past, these types of studies have been limited and they have had mixed results ("Single" par. 2). However, several recent studies that have looked at how well prepared young children are when they enter school reveal encouraging findings. A study cited in Montgomery and Rossi's report concluded, "there is no significant relation between 'family intactness' and degree of risk for educational failure." In this study low-income children with divorced parents are shown to be slightly less likely than low-income children from two-parent homes to be categorized as high risk (par. 1). Another large multiethnic study conducted at Cornell University has found that children from homes with a single mother as the head of the household had no significant disadvantage in school performance solely because of their family structure ("Single" par. 1). Henry Ricciuti, professor emeritus of human development at Cornell states, "Although one-parent families had lower incomes, what mattered most for kids' school readiness was the mothers' ability and educational levels." He also indicates that levels of education and abilities were approximately the same in both of the large samples of single and two-parent families that were analyzed (par. 2). The conclusions of this study suggest that when favorable maternal and household characteristics are present, "single parenthood, in and of itself, is not necessarily a risk factor for children's school readiness" (par. 8).

It would be difficult to argue against the premise that if all other influences are equal, two-parent homes might have a basic advantage in that they could provide more resources and support than single-parent homes. However, the danger lies in making broad generalizations about the severely negative effects of divorce or single-parenthood on children (Montgomery par. 3). It is also counterproductive to cling to an idealized vision of the "traditional family" (Coontz par. 3). Peter Benson and Eugene Roehlkepartain state in their background paper on youth in single-parent families that "two-parent families have an edge, but being in one is no guarantee that a young person will have the nurture, control, and guidance needed to grow up healthy" (par. 2).

Another concept that has been unfairly linked to the structure of the family is "family values." It is often assumed that only two-parent families embody moral values. This assumption, another false generalization, creates a stigma that can have a negative impact on families that do not fit this mold. There is no assurance that someone from a family with two-parents will meet the moral standards set by those who promote these "traditional family values." As Stephanie Coontz points out in her article entitled "The Futility of Teaching Family Values," if one strictly defines "traditional family morality, Mafia families, which condemn premarital sex, abortion, and divorce and value intergenerational loyalty, would score higher than single-parent families or couples with a working mother" (par. 12).

The focus on one family type as the only viable solution to society's problems leads to the misguided assumption that the increase in non-traditional families is a primary cause of these problems. In implying that single parent and blended families are contributing to the degradation of society instead of merely being subject to socioeconomic forces like every other group, political spokespeople are ignoring the real causal factors. Many sociologists and moral leaders have pointed out the flawed reasoning in this supposition. Marian Wright Eldelman voices strong criticism of a society whose leaders "mouth family values they do not practice" (43). Policy-makers consistently vote against legislation which supports the family even though they claim it is their top priority. It is easier to blame non-traditional families for America's problems than to seek long-term solutions. The emphasis on personal responsibility and moral values takes away from an examination of the "broader forces which hurt families, e.g., the impact of economics, discrimination, and anti-family policies" (80).

Some examples of programs which have been repeatedly denied by lawmakers are listed in Eldelman's book, *The Measure of Our Success*. Seventy nations provide financial assistance and medical care to pregnant women—not the United States. Seventeen industrialized nations have programs for paid maternity leave—not the United States (43). A comprehensive childcare bill has been continuously rejected by Congress (44). Although sixty-three other nations provide a family allowance to workers and their children, this is not a program that our government has enacted (45). By failing to invest in programs that protect children and ensure financial stability for working parents, our nation's leaders are undermining all families, especially those with a single parent.

In contrast to this neglect, a strong social support network can serve to reinforce the positive qualities found in families that are considered to be "non-traditional." There are unique strengths found in families with a single parent. The reduction of tensions from a previously high-conflict marriage can result in greater focus on the child's needs and more consistency in the enforcement of rules (Duncan par. 5). Because single parents rely more heavily on the cooperation of their children to keep the family stable, there is a greater potential for interdependence. The children are often more directly involved in problem solving and in making decisions (par. 6). This environment is also more likely to present the opportunity for children to learn new skills (par. 7). When there are two parents to share responsibilities, it is less likely that children will be called upon to contribute to the family's well being. Children in single-parent families may feel more valued because their help is needed on a daily basis (par. 9).

The challenges facing non-traditional families can only be overcome if society does not ignore or blame these groups or stereotype them as abnormal. The true cause of America's social problems has been characterized by Stephanie Coontz as "economics and the culture of selfishness." The solution to these problems does not lie in promoting the superficial and nebulous ideas of "family values" or "the traditional nuclear family," but rather, it can be found in a realistic understanding of the complex issues which are involved. An acceptance of personal responsibility coupled with social and economic support can result in a society that is made up of many different types of viable and healthy family structures.

Works Cited

Benson, Peter L., and Eugene C. Roehlkepartain. "Youth in Single-Parent Families: Risk and Resiliency." *Urban Education Web.* 1993. Columbia University. 4 May 2001 <http://eric-web.tc.columbia.edu/abstracts/ed360462.html>.

Coontz, Stephanie. "The Futility of Preaching Family Values: Economics and the Culture of Selfishness as the Real Root of Social Problems." *The World & I Online* 8 (1994). 1 May 2001 <http://www.worldandi.com/subscribers/1994/August/mt2.cfm>.

Duncan, Steve. "The Unique Strengths of Single-Parent Families." *MSU Communications Services.* Montana State University. 3 May 2001 <http://www.montana.edu/wwwpb/single.html>.

Edelman, Marian Wright. *The Measure of Our Success: A Letter to My Children and Yours.* New York: HarperPerennial, 1993.

Montgomery, Alesia, and Robert Rossi. "Family Characteristics." *Educational Reforms and Students at Risk: A Review of the Current State of the Art.* Jan. 1994. American Institutes for Research. 2 May 2001 <http://www.ed.gov/pubs/EdReformStudies/EdReforms/chap2c.html>.

"Single Motherhood Doesn't Hurt Schoolwork." *EurekAlert!* 27 Sept. 1999. 22 Apr. 2001 <http://www.eurekalert.org/releases/corn-smd092799.html>.

Academic Subject: SOCIOLOGY

This Is Your Brain on TV

by Tommy Denton

TV wages war on our children's minds. It devours their attention and ability to think and make judgments for themselves. In the author's house, the parents are fighting back. Read to find out how.

Probably the most tiresome parental refrain my children have had to endure in their young lives—besides "Clean up your room!"—has been: "No, you can't cook your brains out in front of the TV."

My wife and I didn't even own a television set until our third child was born. While I was visiting the maternity ward before bringing mother and baby home, my own mother called a local dealer and had a set delivered to our house. Grandmothers can be that way.

At any rate, our family joined the TV age.

That was more than 11 years ago, and fighting the great American instinct to flip on the switch seems to have been almost incessant. Although we have relented and allowed rather liberal viewing privileges on Friday nights and Saturday mornings, weekdays and nights are basically off limits for the kids. We make occasional exceptions for particularly informative or otherwise special programs and some family viewing on nonschool nights.

This oppressive restriction has met with plenty of resistance from our children and no small measure of comparison with the more beneficent generosity of their friends' parents.

Which, of course, leads to the zillionth version of our loving admonition that we are not other people's parents, and we care that the children not cook their brains out.

Eyes roll, gasps of exasperation issue forth and young feet shuffle—they have been known to stomp—off to respective bedrooms to while away the remaining hour or so with the obligatory book.

If this is a war being waged for our children's minds, it is a war worth fighting and winning, even though much of American society at times seems to have blissfully surrendered.

In an essay appearing in an edition of the Hillsdale College publication *Imprimis,*, best-selling author Larry Woiwode places television at the core of the demise of one of the essential skills in a republic: the capacity to think.

"Television, in fact, has greater power over the lives of most Americans than any educational system or government or church," Woiwode wrote. "Children are particularly susceptible. They are mesmerized, hypnotized, and tranquilized by TV. No wonder, then, that as adults they are not prepared for the front line of life: they simply have no mental defenses to confront the reality of the world."

Woiwode compares TV with the mythical Cyclops, Polyphemus, encountered by Odysseus in his journeys after the Trojan War. After the war party was trapped in the giant's cave, Polyphemus seized two of Odysseus' men, bashed out their brains and devoured them.

"What I find particularly appropriate about this myth as it applies today is that, first, the Cyclops imprisons these men in darkness, and that, second, he beats their brains out before he devours them," Woiwode wrote. "It doesn't take much imagination to apply this to the effects of TV on us and our children."

The ultimate result, he said, is a destructive erosion of human critical faculties.

"TV eats books. It eats academic skills. It eats positive character traits. It even eats family relationships. TV eats out our substance."

Woiwode referred to observations by Jerry Mander, who wrote the 1978 book *Four Arguments for the Elimination of Television,* citing the numbing effect of television on the ability to differentiate between the real and the unreal.

"(With TV) what we see, hear, touch, smell, feel, and understand about the world has been processed for us," Mander wrote. And when people "cannot distinguish with certainty the natural from the interpreted, or the artificial from the organic, then all theories of the ideal organization of life become equal."

In other words, all images being equal, value judgements about what is good or bad, right or wrong, become irrelevant. That may have some bearing on the results of numerous scientific studies showing a direct relationship between excessive TV viewing and the rising incidence of crime and violence in American society.

The relatively arduous task of reading Dostoevski's *Crime and Punishment*—with its fascinating plot structure, description, character development, and the struggle to fathom the complexities of the human psyche in conflict—is no match for the passive absorption of "Dirty Harry" or "The Terminator."

Once life has been limited to the comfortable, glowing margins of a cathode ray tube and submerged in a pool of hypnotic languor, making sense of life's difficulties, perplexities, joys, and pains hardly seems worth the effort.

At our house we call that cooking your brains out.
